The Club
No One Wanted To Join

Madoff Victims
In Their Own Words

D1453613

Edited by Erin Arvedlund
Compiled by Alexandra Roth

Copyright ©2010 by:

Published by The Doukathsan Press
Of The Massachusetts School of Law
500 Federal Street
Andover, Massachusetts 01810

DEDICATION:

The authors dedicate this book to all the victims of this fraud: direct and indirect investors, union members, charities, foundations and all other affected organizations.

ACKNOWLEDGMENTS:

This book would not have happened if it were not for the unwavering commitment of Erin Arvedlund and Larry Velvel. The authors gratefully acknowledge their tireless efforts and support. Proceeds from the sale of this book will help the victims pursue legislative changes needed to further the rights of the small investor.

Disclaimer

Introduction

What is life like for someone who loses everything? What is the substance of their daily existence a week, a year or more after a tragedy? Do they learn any lessons, or do they not care to learn? Or are they, in fact, surprising everyone by thriving?

No matter what you may think of them, here are the stories of Madoff investors. You are about to hear from regular, mostly middle-class Americans who gave their hard-earned savings to mega-swindler Bernard L. Madoff. Some were completely radicalized by the experience, and have become activists pushing the federal government to help get their money back or simply to expose regulators who failed to catch the $65 billion thief. They warn that the SEC and other regulators could let the same thing happen to you.

Others still carry on in deep shock; and still others found grace in their lives again.

Like a financial serial killer, Madoff knew some of his victims personally. They invested directly by opening up a brokerage account at his seemingly successful brokerage firm. Others had no idea who he was, and invested indirectly, through a bank, a mutual fund, or an arm's length "feeder" fund set up specifically to direct money to Madoff without investors' knowledge. His 10% annual returns didn't seem spectacular—they were atypical of a financial fraud, which gave his victims a sense of comfort.

Most came to Madoff through a referral—a friend, a trusted family member—much like I would ask a confidante for a good doctor, a mechanic or a moving company. Think about it: when was the last time you asked for a referral for something important like your health or your bank account?

But money is a different business altogether, and if Madoff prompted any lesson whatsoever, it is never, ever trust the Securities and Exchange Commission or other of Wall Street's captive regulators to properly guard your finances. They will fail you. Only you can do your own due diligence and accept the results. Also, diversify: It may seem simple but don't put all your money in one bank, one fund, or in one person's care. It's just not worth the risk.

Bernie and his brother Peter and sons Mark and Andrew ran two distinct businesses—a legitimate brokerage firm that was the envy of Wall Street, and a phony hedge fund that was a pyramid, or "Ponzi" scheme, wherein new investors are paid with old investors money (to illustrate, some people argue that Social Security in this country is a Ponzi scheme that will ultimately run out of money over the next several decades; Americans over 65 currently are reaping the benefits of Social Security payments, but with rising costs, younger Americans could actually receive nothing). Bernie claimed they were totally separate businesses, but in fact, in the last years of his crimes, money flowed back and forth between the two operations. It's an important fact because the SEC sniffed around Madoff's operation half a dozen times, and claimed they couldn't find anything. SEC examiners who were suspicious didn't have the power to shut him down.

Currently, the SEC still has not fired anyone for failing to catch Madoff in a lie that ran back several decades. The Obama-appointed SEC Commissioner Mary Schapiro has the world's hardest job. Inherited from a do-nothing Commissioner Christopher Cox. She has reshuffled some divisions and hired former federal prosecutors to make harsh cases against other hedge funds, such as Galleon, but as of yet the SEC still has not made serious reforms inside. To wit, a branch chief in the SEC's Seattle office was recently charged with allegedly surfing the Internet for pornography. He remains employed with the agency.

In my book "Too Good to Be True: The Rise and Fall of Bernie Madoff" (Penguin 2009) I speculate that family members likely knew about and were involved in perpetuating this horrific fraud. Madoff never traded a single stock in his phony hedge fund, and yet his wife, brother, sons and niece collectively withdrew $200 million, at least, in profits. So far, not a single Madoff family member is in jail other than patriarch Madoff, who plead guilty to take the fall and not have to cooperate with authorities. He is serving a 150-year sentence in a North Carolina prison. Some of his henchmen, such as computer programmers and accountants, have been charged with crimes and are awaiting sentencing.

The SEC and other regulators such as FINRA have done nothing for the victims—if anything, they have unleashed a fury over the realization that a fraudster like Madoff can now steal globally. Estimates of the Madoff shockwave are that roughly 3 million people were somehow affected by his fraud, on many continents, in many currencies, and using banks and middlemen as his agents.

The Securities Investor Protection Corp., (SIPC) whose logo brokerage firms pay to print on their statements to gin up a sense of security among retail customers, has also not paid back the bulk of Madoff investors, although the agency was set up under the Nixon administration for the express purpose of protecting Americans who tangle with Wall Street. In a strangely twisted view, SIPC is actually proud to have not helped investors who are victims of Wall Street fraud, including Madoff investors. Is the SIPC logo on your brokerage statement? Probably. Don't expect any money back, even when it's been stolen from you outright.

Many Madoff victims—they prefer to call themselves "survivors" now--are still seeking their back taxes from the federal government in the U.S. Others are in hiding, fearing that the Madoff trustee will come after them for "claw backs", or money the trustee believes they owe to a victims' fund. Insider details about how the system is treating these Madoff investors –and how you could be compensated, or may never be compensated, in a similarly massive or even small financial fraud – will astound you.

9 April 2010
Erin Arvedlund

Post Script

I am pleased to edit this extraordinary series of essays by ordinary people. Alexandra Roth compiled the essays and kept the faith among the writers, and Lawrence R. Velvel, the Dean of Massachusetts School of Law and a professor also, kindly agreed to publish this volume through the university press. Both were Madoff investors. All work for this project was completed on a *pro bono* basis.

TABLE OF CONTENTS

What happens to you does not matter; what you become through those experiences is all that is significant. This is the true meaning of life."
-- <u>author unknown, but whoever you are or were: Thanks.</u>
Sarah Fisk

<u>Part One: Lucky</u>

Did you think you were lucky that you were not ripped off by Bernard L. Madoff? So did I.

In December, 2008, I was standing in my friend's kitchen in Honolulu, Hawaii, when her business manager came in quite upset. His fiancé and her prominent New York family had just lost everything in a huge Ponzi scheme. They said the scope of the fraud was immense, affecting thousands of people and billions of dollars. I thought, "Oh, how awful for them to be caught in a Ponzi scheme. Luckily I know about Ponzi schemes and that would never happen to me. I know my money is safe."

Well, obviously, I was wrong or I wouldn't be writing this. The safe place I had put my money just the year before was a feeder

1

fund to Madoff. I know this now but at that point I had never heard of him. I had taken the advice of my smartest, richest friends and moved my retirement savings to two separate funds (diversify, right?), which I understood to be using a safe, conservative but effective strategy in the stock market. This strategy had been investigated and cleared by the SEC, and had been in place for decades.

That moment in my friend's kitchen still defines this experience for me. When I heard this bad news about others, I felt sympathetic but also a bit superior, as if they must have done something wrong to bring this upon themselves. When I realized that I too had been a victim of this horrendous crime, I felt terrible that I had judged those people. After all, what had I done that most people would not have done in similar circumstances? Nothing.

Back in my hometown of Berkeley, California in the weeks that followed, as I dealt with the reality that my savings had been stolen from me in a very public way, I saw that same judgment in the faces of many people. Mixed in with their sympathy, they were thinking I had made a mistake, or been greedy, or foolish, *unlike* them.

I wanted to be mad at them for this. Especially people in the media, even Daniel Pinkwater of NPR, who blamed Madoff's victims for being greedy, rich, Jewish, or from New York, and thereby somehow deserving to lose their money. But I could not deny that in the days before I knew I was a victim I had felt the same way and had the same judgments. I had thought I was somehow better because it had not happened to me. Seeing this smugness as a basic, thoroughly human reaction rather than an accurate assessment helped me step back. And it got me thinking about luck.

Luck is when we experience something as brought on by chance and/or circumstance rather than by our own actions. (Let's avoid a lengthy philosophical discussion about free will and responsibility by emphasizing that luck is our *experience* of things happening by chance). I have been exposed to a lot of luck lately. Let me fill you in.

In October 2007, my house burned down. Completely. The phrase "I lost everything" came into my vocabulary. It left just as quickly when, a month later, one of my favorite living people was killed in a motorcycle crash. I suddenly realized that all of the precious possessions I had lost in the fire, the lack of a home, and the dissolving of my peace of mind into a bureaucratic jumble of insurance paperwork and destroyed documents, did not constitute losing "everything". I would gladly give up even more if I could have my friend come back to life. I could not.

I was reminded of a favorite Sufi quote, "If you can lose it in a shipwreck, it isn't really yours". The thought that nothing is really "mine", not even my life, helped me see there was a lot I had not lost. I bucked up and counted my blessings. I thought about what mattered to me, spent time with loved ones, and tended to my partner's grief. He had built the house with his own two hands, so he was even more traumatized than I was. We built a new house. It was smaller, not as personal and he didn't like it as much, but I enjoyed the designing and building and couldn't wait to move in and furnish it. I felt the experience had brought us closer as a couple.

So I was genuinely surprised when, two weeks after we moved into the new house, he told me the relationship was over and I would have to leave by the end of the week. After nine years together, he put most of my few remaining possessions into my car and they fit. He waved through his tears as I drove away, then ran after the car to make sure I had given him back his keys.

That was at the end of July 2008. At this point in my life, most people did not think me lucky. But I felt lucky. The realization that I had not "lost everything" led to thinking of all the things I still had. This was so much more interesting and enjoyable than the

3

dismal sense of loss I had experienced that this became my main focus. I won't say I was entirely immune to feelings of grief over what was no more, but I tried to minimize those experiences so as not to interrupt my exploration of the new space that had been created in my life.

This was my frame of mind just a few months later, standing in my friend's kitchen. I was feeling lucky that I still had my savings even though I had lost two houses, most of my worldly possessions and family heirlooms, my cherished relationship, and one of my best friends in a little over a year.

As I think about it now, this frame of mind acted like a vaccine when I found out that I had, also been ripped off by Madoff. Almost all the money I had saved in my adult life had been stolen from me plus a small inheritance: my share of the sale of my mother's house. While my much wealthier friends had much larger sums of money purloined, what was stolen from me amounted to my entire security for my old age. I am currently single and 53 and it looks like I have to start over. Its not that I think this is good, I don't. It's just that when I look around and actually see the world I feel lucky. Things could be worse.

Part Two: Happy

After I found out about Madoff's theft, there was a short period (a month or so) of abject despair during which my beloved uncle was diagnosed with cancer and died. Through this time my normal optimistic outlook was reduced to diagnosable depression. I had intrusive fantasies of the entire global economy collapsing. I imagined needing to scratch out a city garden with my neighbors, augmented with ancient cans of food we could find. I thought I should be hoarding spices and gold and carrying a gun to protect them.

4

I also indulged in some 20/20 hindsight. There were signals. Shouldn't I have known? Back in the day, I had adamantly voted against the elected leaders who dismantled the financial regulatory systems. I knew the fox should not guard the hen house. It did not occur to me that this meant I should not trust the SEC 20 years later, but there it is. Once something has happened, you can see the path that took you there and other paths you didn't take. Analyzing any loathsome event it's natural to look for someone, something, anything to blame but ultimately it may be that all you find is something to learn about yourself.

Following this initial reaction of shock, I realized that I *still* hadn't lost everything. It was one morning as I stood in my living room and felt the air move in and out of my lungs. I looked around me at the physical environment. My stuff, my rented flat built in 1920, the street outside, the trees and the hills in the distance, the clouds in the sky. The logic was obvious: all that had happened was that I had just lost one more thing.

And what was it really that had changed? Numbers on paper. Maybe money is stored up energy, a means of exchange, power to take care of myself and make things happen. Surely I missed this money? What I missed was the feeling of knowing I'd be safe in the future. Had I really known that? Not really. Then I remembered moving into this place many years before. Back then I had no money saved up, I was just starting my career. I hadn't met my partner or moved to Oregon to live with him in his house. Was I happy back then? Well, yes, pretty much. So why not be happy now? A voice in my head started listing all the reasons NOT to be happy now. But just then the sun shone through the window onto my bare feet on the rug and it felt so good and looked so beautiful I started laughing at myself.

Thus began one of the happiest years of my life. It didn't really start until March, but that's okay. There was no stopping it after that. I didn't exactly plan to be happy, either, but I did replace a lot of my internal directives, like "you should do this" or "you should be that", with the simple question: "what would make you happy?" If I received a clear answer, I would just do it. If not, I would hope for the best and pay attention to the situations that I encountered to learn more about what makes me happy.

One of the things I have learned makes me happy is scuba diving. It is like going for a nature walk on another planet. Gravity is different, the atmosphere is different, and the plants and animals are completely "other worldly" even though they are earthlings just like us. I love it.

When you are diving underwater, looking at coral reefs and sea life, one thing that can be very difficult to negotiate is current. The water moves constantly! The more the water is moving the more energy and attention it takes to dive. But all of the creatures in the sea depend upon the movement of water, from tiny coral polyps who only open and feed in flowing water to humpback whales who travel hundreds of miles through the ocean on immense, global currents. Water moves constantly. Even in stillness, water moves.

Life on the land is no different, life moves like water. Life depends on change and change is constant. You can like something or not like it, but it is still going to change. I have a friend who throws her arms wide and says grandly, "Change, it's just the way things are!" And now that I am a diver I say to myself: change is good, like current on a reef.

Am I happy that I had my savings stolen? No. Or that my house burned down, my relationship ended, my friend and my uncle died? No. I am not happy those things happened to me. But at the same time I am glad to be where I am – not in the old house, nor the new one, not with my former partner and open to a new partner, spending time with new friends, loving my family, doing meaningful work, exploring what each day brings.

What has happened has happened. I am still here and those are events of the past. All my favorite spiritual teachers, including the

Dalai Lama, Pema Chodron, Tich Nat Han, Eckhardt Tolle, Byron Katie, seem to agree on something. So do the new brain scientists who can now image brain function and emotion with computers. They all agree that the experience of happiness exists in one place: the present moment. The present moment, which is really all there is. And it is constantly changing.

Let's face it, life is hard and often painful. Sometimes a super powerful current comes along and you get your clock cleaned. But if you survive, as luck would have it, every subsequent moment still brings the chance of happiness. There will always be meaningful work to be done, more fun to be had and lots more people to love.

Rags To Riches, To Rags
Emma De Vita

I am a product of the Great Depression. I learned to never buy anything you cannot pay for, never live beyond your means, and always save for the future.

Shortly after I was born in 1928, my parents packed up the family and moved to Florida. This was to be a new beginning for the family and the start of a new business that would allow my father to support a growing family. There would eventually be ten children. Today, only two survive; I, as the oldest, and my sister, the youngest.

My father made arrangements to run two different businesses in Florida. One was to run an apartment complex named the "Cadillac Apartments." This business was to provide a regular, predictable income for the family. The real prize was to purchase a mahogany Chris Craft speed boat and run it as a tourist attraction. Initially things went well with both businesses and eventually the revenue from the speed boat became the primary source of income for the family.

This ended abruptly when the boat broke down several miles offshore and was towed in by the Coast Guard. There were large swells that day and the boat was broached by a wave and eventually sank. There was no insurance and insufficient money to purchase another boat. Other family issues back home became pressing at about the same time and we again packed up the family; this time moving north back to Philadelphia. At this point the family consisted of two children.

We moved to an apartment in Philadelphia and my father got a job working for a contractor that painted homes. This is when the family really started to grow. A new child was born every two years. As the family grew we moved several time to larger quarters – always as renters. With the larger family came more pressure on income. The oldest kids took local jobs cleaning horse stalls, collecting roadside metals that could be sold to a junk yard and selling flowers that we grew ourselves and pastries that my mother made in her kitchen.

My father wanted one more opportunity to start his own business. Taking our savings we once again packed up the family and move to Franklinville, New Jersey, where my father leased a farm and purchased several thousand chickens. We needed six months to allow the chickens to grow to a sufficient size to sell. We almost made it. Just a few weeks before our "sell date", the chicken coup became infested with a disease that killed half the chickens. We lost the farm and moved back to Philadelphia. There were now six children.

World War II came along and my father got a job working at the Frankford Arsenal in Philadelphia making munitions for the war effort. The eighth child came along. This new child was born with mental issues, became very sick and nearly died. While he did recover, he was never able to function as a normal adult. His treatment by the school system, government and society in general was much different that what someone with his disability would face today.

My father changed jobs again as the war approached the midway point. He worked in the paint shop at the Philadelphia Navy Yard and received a significant increase in salary. This increase was absolutely necessary as the family continued to grow.

I was now 14 and permitted to leave school to help with family finances. In those days, children went to work and brought their money home to the father of the household – all of it. I was given a small allowance, but the real objective of my quitting school and working was to support the younger children in the household.

The Second World War was fast approaching a successful conclusion. Things were looking bright for the family. Then my father started to have stomach problems. Over the next few years we had a series of trips to doctors. But my father never really seemed to get better. He passed away in 1947 from cancer that was never clearly diagnosed or treated.

The tenth child was born weeks before my father passed away. I was 19.

The burden for supporting ten kids fell upon my mother, the widow, and the oldest children. The objective became to make the most money you could regardless of whether you liked the job or not. I started to work at a factory. My oldest brother went to work at Bond Bread and my mother worked on assembling TV sets.

It was at Bond Bread that my brother met several returning veterans who recently started working at the company. One of these vets eventually became my husband of 60 years. It truly was love at first sight. Most men would have run the other way when he saw a family with 10 kids and a widow. My husband did not. He was an instant hit with the older kids and a sensation with the younger ones. He talked of getting married in two months and asked me if it would be okay to have a large family. He came from a family of eight. After the experience of being "the mom" for my younger brothers and sisters at the age of only 14, I told him that "if you want a large family, then you need a different girl." Again, he did not run away.

We married in 1949 and bought a small house near my mom. My first child was born fifteen months after we got married. Just as in the past, my younger brothers and sisters became our extended family. Our own children, plus this extended family became the "large" family that my husband always wanted.

My husband's family was "wealthy." They had a small 600 sq ft home in Wildwood Villas and we spent many happy years in that home playing cards, catching and cooking crabs with spaghetti and growing a little vegetable garden.

Things were going extremely well. My mother's kids were now all grown up and I was beginning my own family. The job at Bond Bread seemed secure (after all, people would always eat bread) and my husband was now a shop foreman.

There was still a draft in place and all of the men on both sides of the family were either drafted or joined the military. My husband's father was one of the "doughboys" who volunteered to fight for the allies in World War I. He eventually would serve in the trenches outside of Paris and received the Purple Heart for wounds received during one offensive.

Then along came the Cold War, Korea and Vietnam. Members of my family served in every U.S. conflict from WWI right through the Gulf War. You will recognize the names of some of the places and battles where they fought including Guam, Saipan, Bastogne, Inchon, Khe-Sahn, Fallujah, and the Atlantic convoys transporting war materials from the U.S. to Britian. Our men served as riflemen, MPs, sailors, electricians, airmen and paratroopers. None were officers; all were regular Americans who did their duty when called

11

to serve. With the exception of my sixty year old son who served as a Naval airman, all of our personal "heroes" are now gone.

By this time I moved from Philadelphia to the suburbs. My daughter moved there just a few months earlier and I, like my mother, wanted to be near my children and grandchildren.

Life was grand. After 22 years working for Sears, I quit and went to work in my son's business.

In the early 1990's my son discussed a new investment opportunity and we both opened an account with a firm named Avellino and Bienes. In 1992 this was converted to an account with Bernard Madoff Investment Securities following an SEC investigation that led to the closure of the Avellino and Bienes firm and the implied recommendation that Madoff was a very well respected money manager and that his firm was one of the largest in the NASDAQ.

Beginning in 1998 my husband and I started to travel. I had never flown before and had a great fear of getting into an airplane. My daughter and son-in-law scheduled a family trip to Florida and we went along. I took a nerve pill and got on the airplane – one shaky step at a time. It was absolutely an exhilarating experience. Flying opened up a whole new world. In the next four years we traveled to Alaska, California and the Caribbean.

We were getting older now – and no one lives forever. Our goal was that this investment account would be used to replace the income from social security and pension for the one who passed first. I thought that would be me. My husband was absolutely NEVER sick.

It is now 2002 and our future and retirement looks very secure. My husband retired from his job as the building superintendent at the YMCA, and my grandchildren were in the process of starting their own families. We decided to set 2005 as our final retirement year and begin to live on our investment with Madoff.

But as always, fate plays a part in every life. Even the best laid plans, no matter how well thought out, are subject to human fragilities. In early 2004 my husband got quite ill. This was eventually diagnosed as multiple myeloma – which is incurable. The next few years were a whirlwind of doctors, tests and treatment. The medication of choice to treat his cancer was thalidomide (yes the old drug from the 50's that was initially used for pregnant women). It was VERY expensive, costing more than $5,000 per month. This was a complex disease. I kept a loose leaf folder where I recorded notes for every doctor seen, every test taken, every medication prescribed, every hospital visit and every operation. The book eventually grew to over 300 pages and I firmly believe that the information in this book that tied all of these various entities together extended my husband's life and reinforced my understanding of the disease. In 2007 we made our one and only withdrawal from the Madoff account – to pay for medical bills. Eventually, in 2008 my husband succumbed to the disease and he passed away.

The time had come to implement "the plan." Over the course of the next seven months my family and I completed the necessary paperwork to finalize my husband's estate. On December 8, 2008, I was in the office of my local bank arranging to close the Madoff account and begin living on the income from a two decade investment. It was not meant to be.

Although my son found out about the Madoff arrest late in the evening of December 11, 2008, he did not tell me about it for three more days. I believe he was trying to spare me the pain of knowing that my life would never be the same and that the goals and plans discussed years ago would never come to pass.

I simply could not believe that all those brokerage account statements, stock transaction statements and 1099s reporting all my "earnings" were nothing more than tissue paper.

Madoff, the monster, had stolen my life.

Now, rather than "living the plan", I live with a dramatically different lifestyle with very different objectives and with a very different "job."

My new "job" is communicating with others who were victimized by Madoff to attempt to recover some small portion of my investment. A significant part of my remaining income, which is largely Social Security, is devoted to accountants and attorneys who advise me about things that need to be done to address the Madoff fraud. I cannot spend my entire limited income on myself – I continue to spend way too much on Madoff.

I spend hours each week on the phone with legislators in an attempt to recover the major source of monies available to me – taxes paid for two decades on fraudulent 1099 income. I simply cannot understand how the government can keep this money. Only a morally bankrupt society would keep taxes collected as a result of a criminal activity.

I spend hours reading the news items that describe in sickening detail the role that the SEC played in allowing Madoff to perpetrate this fraud for so long.

And, I hope and pray, that our elected legislators "come through" for us and do the right and moral thing. Our government played a huge role in perpetuating the Madoff fraud and they need to do all they can to make it right.

My life has changed in a number of ways, none of which could have been imagined in 1990, 1992 or even 2008 when my husband passed.

> I wanted to put central air in my home to make it more appealing when I sell it.

14

I wanted to buy a hybrid car to replace the one that my husband routinely drove.

I shop with coupons and check all the ads before I buy something.

It is cheaper to go the second hand store to buy clothes.

I turn the thermostat down and sit near an electric heater so I do not have to heat the entire house.

I am 81 – my years are coming to an end. I will have little if anything left in my estate to pass along to my heirs

In some ways I am one of the fortunate Madoff investors. I still have my very supportive family. Thank God for the Madoff group. It has been not just a source of information but also a source of inspiration. Like most in the group, I find myself supporting the objectives of others just because it is the right thing to do, not because it will benefit me personally.

I may have lost my money, but I am still rich.

I want my fellow Americans to gain a better understanding of what the real Madoff investor looks like. You need to understand that we did nothing wrong other than listening to the agency that is tasked by congress with protecting me against this type of fraud. So far, my country, through the SEC, has failed me. I hope that your country will not fail you.

My story is that of the typical American family – just like the story you would be telling me about your family.

I have a message for you – and I hope you are willing to listen.

It Was All a Lie – **Bernie, the Securities and Exchange Commission and Securities Investors Protection Corporation**
Timothy Murray

It's a Rumor

After almost driving off the road I calmed down realizing it was yet another rumor. We were due for one. It seems that they come around every so often and are investigated by the Securities and Exchange Commission and found to be untrue.

I knew that over the years Madoff's trading strategy had been questioned, investigated by the Securities and Exchange Commission and the brokerage industry's own regulatory agency the Financial Industry Regulatory Authority, and given a clean bill of health, multiple times. I chalked all that nonsense up to jealousy by other Wall Street traders. No other trader was investigated with the regularity that Madoff was. This should have made him the most trusted trader on Wall Street.

He was the former Chairman of the NASDAQ stock exchange and

had been on Wall Street since 1960. In a man there was no one alive that personifies Wall Street other than Bernard L. Madoff. I am supposed to believe that one day he gets up in the morning and does something to get arrested for? Not likely.

I had managed commercial, residential buildings, land and other financial aspects for the family for the last 20 years. I dealt with people at the Madoff firm on a quarterly basis and with Madoff himself personally once or twice a year. The last time I spoke to him it was in relation to estate tax planning. We actually implemented one of his recommendations. Little did we know that he had already implemented his own plan for the estate.

Sleepless Night

By morning I had read everything there was to read about Madoff on the Internet and I had the Securities Investor Protection Corporation on speed dial. I hit the button at 8:00 AM and was relieved to hear that Madoff was a member in good standing of the Securities Investor Protection Corporation and that the SIPC logo on the statements and trade confirmations we had received for decades was not a lie too. I briefly described the accounts we had including one account with two customers and one with eleven customers. The very nice lady said that the insurance coverage was per account, not per customer. I said, "But your website and downloadable brochure says customers." She responded that their attorneys have advised them to change that. But, but... Well, at least the family will be able to recover a portion of the money invested, I thought.

The Lipstick Building

In the early '90s I was in New York City visiting my son at college and I called Frank DiPascali, Madoff's right-hand man, and told him I was in town and would like to see the operation. I was aware that Bernard L. Madoff Investment Securities was a major player and an innovator, in electronic trading, executing trades and accepting order flow for other Wall Street traders, amounting to a significant daily volume and that they made markets in a select number of stocks. To me this was like attending the Super Bowl and the World Series at the same time.

"Hello, Tim from Minnesota calling, I am in the City and would love to see your offices!"

Frank: "Well, what do you want?"

Me: "I would just like to see your offices, you know and shake hands."

Frank: "Well how long do you think that will take?"

Me: "Not long just want to say hello and see the trading floor."

Frank: "Well, ok then."

I met Frank DiPascali at the Lipstick Building and was key carded onto the trading floor. Grays and blacks for the interiors, very impressive and elegant in an understated way.

On the trading floor itself there were maybe 20 traders sitting at desks all in their twenties, and thirties, tapping their keyboards. I have been in libraries that were more clamorous – no phones ringing – no one shouting – no hand signals and no discarded trade slips on the floor. Just the tapping of keyboards making money. Every trader did have an uncradled telephone receiver on his desk and nothing else except for a flat screen monitor. While I was standing there, taking it all in, someone walked over to one of the traders and tapped him on the shoulder and pointed to the receiver. The trader picked it up and discussed something very important.

Off to one side was a platform built-up higher than the trading floor

18

with three desks. Each had flat screen monitors and three older looking traders manned those desks. I asked Frank what their function was and he said, "Looking for mistakes". Remarkable, I was witnessing the future of securities trading through the efficiency of computers and we were a part of it!

All this time Frank looked pensively at the trading ticker on the wall. I wondered why he looked so stressed. Madoff's split-strike conversion made money on the stock market moving – up or down. If the long positions went up the options expired worthless, a small price to pay for the security of protecting the longs. If the long positions went down the option contracts covered the loss and more. Why was he so stressed?

Three Generations

In 1925, Boyer, a Swedish immigrant came though Ellis Island in his mother's arms, the family later settled in Minnesota where his father had gone previously to establish himself.

At 16 years of age Boyer became a plaster's apprentice, working alongside his father, and attending school at night to earn his high school diploma. Later, he started a small plastering company and from there transitioned into a completely new and revolutionary wall system, eventually becoming a major Midwest drywall contractor, employing thousands over its 50 year history. His sons and grandchildren continue the tradition in the drywall business today.

Boyer and Fern were married when they were 18 years old and are still married after almost 70 years. Boyer considers her his most valuable asset. Money was so tight for this young couple that a typical dinner in the apartment they shared with another couple was boiled hot dogs and soup. They called the soup wiener water soup, not wanting to waste.

They went on to have five children; those children provided them with eleven grandchildren. The family had accounts at Madoff for their education, and to give them a start in life. They also progressively increased their charitable giving as the years passed. Boyer recently donated his retirement account to a local nonprofit for their new building project.

The Investment

Boyer knew a local Minnesotan named Mike Engler from his teenage years and later made his first investment of $1,000 in the stock market with Engler's brokerage firm. That was a substantial amount of money for him at the time. The investment went well so when Mike approached him about investing with Bernard Madoff, the former Chairman of the NASDAQ stock exchange, years later, he was receptive. As Boyer recalls the first investment started out small and after a number of years, after the investment had proved out, he moved his retirement account to Madoff. Over the decades that followed when he sold land or commercial buildings much of the proceeds were deposited in his account at Bernard L. Madoff Investment Securities.

More Than A Year Has Passed

The eighteen family members were 15 to 87 years old when Madoff confessed and turned himself in December 2008. They are now a year older and at varied stages in life; school, college, jobs, near retirement and retirement. It is difficult for them to understand how the Government could have failed them and continues to fail them so completely and inscrutably.

For the very first time in SIPC's 40-year history it is refusing to pay claims based upon the Customer's last statement. One of the reasons that Congress created SIPC through the enabling legislation of the Securities Investors Protection Act was to give investors confidence in relying on registered brokers that are SIPC members. Another significant reason was that it allowed for brokers to hold securities purchased for a customer in their own name, colloquially referred to as Street Name. This has saved Wall Street massive amounts of money in eliminating the overhead involved in titling stock in Customer's name but increased the risk to the investing public. This risk was offset by the enactment of SIPA insuring each Customer up to $500,000.

In the liquidation of New Times Security Services, Inc., another Ponzi scheme, Steven Harbeck, President of SIPC, testified:

Mr. HARBECK: Even if they're not there.

THE COURT: Even if they're not there.

MR. HARBECK: Correct.

THE COURT: In other words, if the money was diverted, converted-

MR. HARBECK: And the securities were never purchased.

THE COURT: Okay.

MR. HARBECK: And, if those positions triple, we will gladly give the people their securities positions.

New Times was a very small, $30 million Ponzi scheme. SIPC paid the customers based on their last statement even though the money was stolen and the stocks were never purchased. Maybe size does matter.

Mary Schapiro, Chairwoman of the Securities and Exchange Commission, testified that, "The tragic truth is that there is not enough money available to pay off all of the customer claims". My sense of this is that it is because the member brokers have not paid premiums for the last nineteen years and the SEC failed in their mission to protect investors by not detecting the Madoff fraud, even after it was gift wrapped and handed to them by Harry Markopolos, multiple times, over a period of many years.

Steven Harbeck, the President of SIPC testified that it would take another year just to determine all of the claims, although the statute says to promptly pay claims. There is no mention of launching multiyear forensic accounting investigations costing one million dollars per week. He also testified that the Trustee is not going to sue innocent small investors – "We will invite them to enter into discussions." I am assuming it's not to talk about baseball scores.

What Can American Citizens Invest In?

A national securities firm I spoke to, post Madoff, has a Lloyds of London policy for 150 million per customer in addition to the SIPC coverage to protect their customers, that's very impressive, but what does it mean? On closer reading of the Lloyds coverage it says, "As defined by the SIPC rules". We declined the investment.

What about the Federal Deposit Insurance Corporation, will they pay bank customers if there is a clever thief, say an insider at the bank stealing over a long period of time? Are the bank regulators doing a better job of regulating the banks than the SEC does regulating the securities industry? If your stockbroker's statement cannot be relied on, can your bank statement be relied on?

Madoff could not have committed this fraud without the Securities and Exchange Commission and Securities Investors Protection Corporation. The SEC and SIPC were integral to the scheme. The twin illusions that the SEC was protecting customers from dishonest registered brokers and that their customers would be protected by the industry funded SIPC insurance, allowed him to steal billions from thousands of people.

If Wall Street's SIPC is allowed to wriggle out of paying these claims the American Taxpayer will be bailing out Wall Street once again. No one, not even the Trustee, spending one million dollars per week on forensic accounting, knows the final figures but it is reasonable to believe that thousands of direct customers will amend their tax returns to correct Appendix A, Line 8, Potential insurance/SIPC recovery, of what is commonly referred to as Safe Harbor Rules. This will cause the United States Treasury to issue refunds and or loss carry forwards amounting to hundreds of millions of dollars. As of this writing the exact amount that Wall Street is attempting to shift to the Taxpayer is unknown.

Boyer and Fern were 87 years old when Madoff confessed and said, "It was all a lie." and turned himself in. They have not heard anything from the Trustee regarding the status of their claims. They are now 88 years old and wonder if they will be here to see the issues resolved.

Madoff and the decades long failures of Securities and Exchange Commission was the earthquake – The continuing failure of the Securities Investor Protection Corporation to pay customer claims is the tsunami that is wreaking havoc on thousands of people.

It was all a lie.

What Can I Tell You About Myself, Other Than I Lost $30,000 To Madoff?

R.V.

I'm a 32 year old, mixed race, self-employed woman who has taken care of myself since a very young age. I have been very careful about my money since I saw the correlation between money and freedom. To me, freedom is priceless.

I was abandoned by my mother when I was six years old, a few weeks after my father left and took both of my brothers with him. My mom blamed me for his leaving. For the next four years I was passed around my family like I was a hot Maryjane cigar. I missed out on school for those four years since my uncle decided that I'd be good for house cleaning, babysitting his rotten kids and taking care of my sick-crippled grandmother which I didn't mind because she taught me so much. She taught me how to be headstrong and have some self-respect and not let anybody pre-determine what my life is going to be other than what I wanted it to be.

After that, I ended up bouncing around group homes until the age of eighteen when I got my freedom. In some of those group homes I was always told that I was never going to amount to anything other than being a welfare mom with god knows how many kids or a crack head hooker who's probably going to end up dead or in jail. I didn't like any of those options.

I knew I wanted to become independent, I just didn't know how. I started working in restaurants and warehouses, and even picked tobacco leaves in the summer. I realized I needed a trade. So I went to trade school. I worked really hard to pay for it. At minimum wage it wasn't enough so I practically became homeless. I became a professional truck driver, moved in to the rig and started working. In a field dominated by men I had to work extra hard to prove my worth.

Then I discovered tourism! Tourism workers made a good living. So I jumped right in head-first. I got to travel all over the place! It felt good to practically get paid to go on vacation. I started saving money for retirement. I knew that I wanted to invest my money I just didn't know how. I don't have a college or financial education and the only math I learned at those group homes was on how to balance a checkbook and write checks to pay bills! Not to mention the importance of how many hours I need to work a week at minimum wage in order to pay rent!!! Yeah!!! Wohoo!!!

Then, I met a good friend of mine who ran an investment group and was teaching me about investing money. It felt good to invest, I felt like my money was working for me too.

I know that $30,000 is just chump change for most people in the investment world, but for me, it was my life savings. I worked hard for it! Nobody gave me anything. I didn't go on public assistance of any sort; it was a matter of pride and self-respect for me. I was homeless for about two years working hard to pay for my classes. But it's okay. I am not going to cry about it. What's done is done. I started this rat race with nothing. And now I am a Jane of all trades. And in this great country of ours, opportunity and possibilities are endless. I'm older now with more life experience and a whole slew of skills. I do it all and if I haven't done it before I'm willing to try.

One of the things I love doing is woodworking. I would like to find an apprenticeship with a yacht refinishing company and do woodworking on yachts as a seasonal, part-time job each fall here in south Florida. I find the work therapeutic. In the meantime, my business partners and I have "all hands on deck". We have in the past and currently still fix up properties and either rent them out or sell them outright for a profit. I know we will be successful in real estate again or whatever else we happen to get into. We did it once. We'll do it again. We never got in over our heads. We never failed.

Madoff took it from us. One thing I can guarantee is that this time around we will be much more appreciative and in many ways much more successful!

I've been beaten down in many ways in my life before and I have survived it all. So if all of the negative circumstances in my life didn't finish me when I had nothing and no one... Neither is this douche bag Madoff!

My family and I are going to get through this and bounce right back--and I'm not talking about the family I was born into. I had to let go of them and their abusive and destructive ways. Only a handful of people are lucky enough to be born into a true loving family and the rest of us aren't; that's just life. It is up to us to figure out how happy and successful we truly want to be. No one can give us that but ourselves. We have to look deep inside ourselves and make peace and let go of the things that oppress us. As painful as that may be, sometimes you just have to let things and people go. Some people you simply have to stay away from, the Madoffs of the world. They have no soul!

It's up to us to decide how we want to live our lives. We can choose to break free from that abusive and oppressive cycle or just wallow in it. The fact of the matter is that we write our own destiny. My new family includes the two best friends a person could ever have in the world. These are the two people who have been there with me through thick and thin. They were my cheerleaders when I was down, my strength when I was weak. I am as committed to them as much as they are to me and that's the true definition of a family to me. We will continue to succeed personally and financially.

And what will I do with the part of the profits that I would've probably sent to Madoff? When that fateful day does arrive, this time I'll stuff my money in my mattress. In this day and age I think it's safer that way.

This is not a movie, or is it? If it is then like most movies, it opens up with the happy scene, the scene where everything is going great- an upper middle class Jewish-American family, three generations strong, living the American dream.

Growing up in a nice house in a nice suburb, our parents made sure my siblings and I got the best education available. Surviving grandparents were being taken care of; they lived in Florida. I am the third generation, along with my brother and sister. I graduated from high school in New Jersey and went to College in New Hampshire and law school in Manhattan. I lived in Manhattan for nine years practicing law, and I loved it there. I never wanted to be one of those bridge-and-tunnel people who worked in the City and commuted home to New Jersey everyday- for me, it was Manhattan or nothing at all.

For six years, I worked at a prestigious law firm on Wall Street, specializing in corporate law and mergers and acquisitions, and for six years I made good money. I was never one to buy name-brand things, simply for the sake of having name-brand things. I was practical. I thought more about working hard now, saving and investing my money for the future. I was planning on moving to Florida where I would get a government job- of course, I would be sacrificing the Wall Street money, but at the same time I would not have the Wall Street pressure. With this plan in mind, I saved every dime that I could and planned for my future in sunny South Florida.

One year after getting a sizeable year-end bonus, I asked my father's opinion on how or where he thought I should invest my money to yield the best returns- after all my father was in sales and finance, and as far back as I could remember, we never had any money problems. My brother, sister and I all went to college on his dime because he wanted all his children to have a private education.

I also knew that my father and uncle invested and they were satisfied with their returns, but I didn't know with whom or in what they invested. My father said to me "put your money with Madoff, because he invests in quality and well-known securities and has been given a clean bill of health by the Feds over the years." As for me, this was the first time I was hearing about Bernie Madoff (and if this was a movie, it would be the introduction of the bad guy, but this bad guy has been good for years). I quizzed my father about what he knew about Madoff's investments, and he told me that years earlier he attempted to ask Bernie about his investment strategies. At that time, Bernie simply told him that if he didn't trust him, he could just pull out of the investment entirely. There were plenty of investors clawing to invest with Bernie!

My dad trusted Madoff. My uncle trusted my dad- he and his family also invested with Madoff. We trusted our dad, so my sister, brother and I invested with Madoff, and for years everything was great. My father was no longer putting money in the account- he has long since retired, living off the interest on the account balance. My brother, sister, and I were depositing money because we wanted our money to grow, and we liked the security of knowing that Madoff was a well-known, trusted and respected brokerage firm.

I had plans of my own: remember my cushy government job in Florida? I had plans to buy a house when I moved to Florida and intended to put down a sizeable down payment using my Madoff savings. So, I decided to leave the hustle and bustle of New York City in 2005 and moved to Miami for a stint with a university. By that time my parents had also migrated to Florida. Growing tired of Miami, I moved to Palm Beach County in 2008 to be closer to my family and away from the insane Miami lifestyle.

At this point, everything was going as planned. I had migrated to Florida, close to my parents and grandparents in the Boca Raton area. I found the house I wanted to buy, paid a portion of the down-payment out-of-pocket, intending to pay the balance of the down-payment with funds from my Madoff account.

It is as vivid in my mind as if it was yesterday. One day in early December, after leaving my cushy government job I went by my parents' house, and they were in the living room watching television. It's as if they were waiting for me to walk through the door. Immediately they told me that they needed to talk to me, and my first thought was "Oh my god, who died?" It was like when you were young and you did something wrong, and as soon as you walk in the house they said "young lady we need to talk", and your heart drops and you think "oh s---t, how did they find out?!" Well, I had not done anything wrong. Furthermore, I was not that little girl anymore. I no longer got chastised. I was an independent, do-as-I-please, when-I-please and if-I-please, successful young attorney. So I thought "who died?!" Within the seconds that seemed like hours, I thought of all the people that I did not want it to be, which was pretty much all my family- my parents did not know my friends, so it had to be a family member.

With all these thoughts going through my mind, and not wanting to hear the bad news, and I knew it was bad news because by now I saw the looks on both their faces, and it was not the "young lady we need to talk look". It was "something really bad has happened, and we don't know how to tell you" look. I am very close to my parents; my mother is my best friend. She's the one that I go to for advice when I am in doubt, when my boyfriends used to tell me that I am a spoiled brat, she's the one that would tell me "baby, you're not a spoiled brat, you just choose not to settle for less, and if they don't understand that, then they're not deserving of you." My father would always agree with my mother, but it seemed like he was never really convinced. I sometimes felt that when they were alone at night, he would say to my mother "she is a spoiled brat, but I'd never tell her that".

I have been around these two people all my life. I knew all their looks. I have been seeing these looks from kindergarten to elementary to middle school, through high school and college and law school, but this look- this look I had never seen before.

"Take a seat," my dad said. Now my mind conjured up a million thoughts like "this s--t is definitely serious, it's one of those 'take a seat talks'". I have had very few of those over the years. I prefer being chastised. As I sat down, I glanced at my mother sitting down staring at the television as if she was in a trance, and then it hit me. He found out that I'm dating outside the religion, and this it's going to be one of those talks like "baby we're not racist, but you need to find yourself a nice, Jewish boy," or "baby, you have to think about the family, and your heritage." I prepared myself for that talk.

Well, you know what, this comes to an end today. I'll date whoever I want to date, whatever color, whatever religion. I am so tired of this garbage. You know what, bring it on Dad, because this is going to end quicker than a Mike Tyson fight. I am a grown woman and I will not be subjected to being sat down and being told who I should date and who I should not date. Now I know why my Mom is sitting over there with her back turned to us. She wants no part of this. Normally, I can always count on her support, but I guess she feels she really cannot support me on this, so I guess I'm on my own, but you know what, I can handle it. As a matter of fact, I'm glad we're doing this because this has been bothering me for a while, and it's about time I get this chip off my shoulder….

The money is gone!!!

While I was busy planning my attack, I saw my dad's lips move and I thought I heard him say "the Money is Gone!!!" Hold on, let me collect my thoughts, the Money is Gone? What the hell is he talking about, what money? This talk is not about me dating the wrong men. I'm glad, actually, because I really don't want them to be disappointed in me…. As he spoke, he pointed to the television. Madoff just got arrested, his sons turned him in, it's on the news:

The Money is Gone!!!

As I turned, I saw my mother still sitting there, still in a trance-like state. I didn't know what to think or what to say or do.

30

Now I understood the looks on their faces. This is far worse than anything I would have thought of in a million years. As we sat there in silence looking at the images on the television, I couldn't help but think about my dad and what he must be going through-not only has he just discovered that his retirement money is gone, but the money to pay off the house is gone, the car insurance, paying Grandma's bills, everything is gone, and if that wasn't enough, the guilt he must be feeling for subjecting his children to the same fate.

I felt his pain and his guilt in my own way. For once in my adult life, I felt helpless. I felt powerless, and it was a feeling I didn't like. Wall Street teaches you to be tough, because it's a dog-eat-dog world. It's not a place for the tired or the weak-hearted. Not only did I survive on Wall Street, I was the big dog. On Wall Street, I protected my clients' interests every day. I protected them from harm. I would go to battle for my clients, without regard for the opposition and without a doubt that I would be victorious-because I had no fear. With fear, you have lost the war before the battle has even begun. So, where was I when my dad needed me to go to battle for him? Where was I when he needed protection? Where was I when the man who put me through school on his own dime and has never asked me for anything in return....where was I when he needed me? I can't help but feel responsible, as if there is something I should have been able to do for him, for my family, even for myself.

Even though we are all affected, I feel as if I am indebted to my father and that I need to repay every dime that was stolen from him and from my family, or at least fight the battle on his behalf and on behalf of the others like him that were blindsided in this tragedy. For the younger generation like myself, my brother and sister, it's a big setback and disappointment, but we have time to rebound. The older generation of investors does not have the time to rebound. This was their everything- these people did not put their lifesavings in Bank of America- they put it in the protection and trust of Bernie Madoff, and he betrayed them.

As we sat there in frozen silence, and I saw the look of hopelessness and despair on my parents' face, the tears started coming, uncontrollable tears. I have heard people talk about an out-of-body experience....for me, this was it, because this s---t can't be real. It must be a movie or something, but if it is a movie who the hell is the director, because this plot doesn't make any sense . . . everybody knows that Jews do not steal from Jews- it's an unwritten rule since the beginning of time- that is why Jewish communities thrive anywhere in the world . . .so, where the hell is the director to tell these actors not to ad lib, because they do not understand the Jewish culture. Just follow the f—king script! Nowhere in the script does it say that Jews steal from other Jews!

Now let's shoot that scene again, and this time, let's get it right- no more talk of betrayal or mistrust or stealing peoples' life savings, now let's go....

Lights- Camera-Action!!!

True Wealth – The Gifts of Devastation
Mary Thomajan

I have thought about all of the ways I could begin this story … but what keeps coming to my mind is a conversation I had with my father during his dying days with cancer. The disease had taken its toll on both of my parents and the atmosphere was heavy; I found myself asking him if he could recall the time when he fell in love with my mother. His eyes brightened and his frail body smiled as he remembered his love for her, his ardent pursuit, and his promise to marry her and "show her the world".

Their first assignment was post-war Germany, and things there were pretty grim there. My mother chimed in next to describe what it was like to arrive in a foreign country for the very first time with a trainload of young American brides – at the tender age of 18:

> *"Our train pulled into a station that had been bombed into rubble… there were no buildings, just a huge pile of rocks…. and standing there in the middle of all of that devastation was the most gorgeous hunk I had ever seen ….. It was your father".*

I will never forget those words, because they spoke to me of hope in the face of despair, of new life and new promise emerging from death and destruction, of the nature of change and the power of love to transform our history and our experience.

Love knows that experience is temporary.

Love knows that there are no ordinary moments.

My journey on this earth has been anything but ordinary. I have traveled to the outer edges of the planet, and within, to the innermost depths of my being. You could say that I have lived several lives within this one, but for this chapter, allow me to fast-forward to fall of 2008.

For some time, with a quiet but growing excitement I have been salting away my savings for that day when I would design and build my dream home in the mountains of Santa Fe, New Mexico, where under that brilliant cobalt blue sky, I would live a life filled with love, art, beauty, peace and service. I had a dream to start a foundation for worthy projects or a Center for Community and Courageous Change. I somehow knew that I wanted to help people move fearlessly through the massive changes that are coming to our planet.

Well, that day had finally arrived. I had enough to step into my new future and I was making plans to move to New Mexico in the summer of 2009.

I had it all worked out in my mind.

I must not have had it quite worked out in my heart however, because in late fall of 2008 I found myself in daily prayer, pleading to be shown how I could weave all my gifts and experience into a living tapestry that was at once coherent, authentic and beautiful – one that could serve, transform and inspire others. In other words, I prayed to be *wholly revealed* – to illuminate my purpose and my contribution to Creation.

I stood there in my living room and commanded the angels, "I'm ready! Send me my Dharma, now!"

Then I boarded a plane to India.

That December 2008, just one day following my return, my Dharma arrived – on the fax machine.

I thought it was the year-end report that would seal my imminent dream. Instead, floating halfway down a blank white page, as if dashed off hastily by the sender, a cryptic paragraph in 9pt type read:

> "Bernard Madoff, founder of Bernard L. Madoff Investment Securities LLC, was arrested today in New York by federal authorities for perpetrating a massive securities fraud, alleged to have involved losses of 50B in what may be described as a giant Ponzi scheme. Our fund which has substantially all of its assets invested with Madoff is a victim of this fraud. ... At this point, it is impossible to predict what recovery, if any, may be had on these assets."

That was it. No phone call, no explanation or consolation, no further information. Eighteen years of investment history up in smoke (and mirrors). I stared dumbstruck at the page, expecting it to dissolve as I woke from a dream.

I read it again slowly, and this time I experienced a fleeting but unmistakable sense of relief ... just long enough to hear my mind form the thought ... *Good – now I don't have to worry about that anymore....*

For a brief instant I was in touch with the burden and responsibility that wealth had conveyed: managing and monitoring, the incessant search to find trustworthy and competent advisors and managers, the trail of forms and paperwork, tracking and filing the taxes, the looming specter of responsible stewardship, planning for the transfer to the heirs, the perpetual re-balancing, reinvesting and moving it around, and the worst part --- *living with the constant fear of losing it.* This is contractive energy.

Those who believe that individuals with money have no problems have never had any money. Wealthy people just have a different set of problems.

My mind snapped back to the present moment, struggling against this inconceivable new reality: *'There must be some mistake! This cannot be right. Surely this is not what I prayed for! I saved all these years. I was prudent. I invested. I had a plan. I didn't live extravagantly. I am a good person. I gave money to worthy causes every year. I was on the cusp of my life's dream!'*

In the 50 seconds it took to read that fax, I went from being a multi-millionaire to having my life savings wiped out and life as I knew it forever altered. Life *as I knew it.*

As my new circumstances began to sink in, *terror* gripped my being and a million survival questions roiled in my mind.

I obsessed: How will I manage my mortgages and bills? Will I need to sell my home? Can I sell my home in the current depressed market? Should I get a new job, or try to quickly build my fledgling businesses into an income that can cover my bills and living expenses? Who would hire me at this age in this economy? Should I try to start a new business and how would I fund that? Will I see any of this money ever again? What about the taxes I paid for twenty years on money that didn't exist? Am I eligible for insurance? How am I going to figure all this out? How am I going to get the information? I can't afford an attorney. What are my rights as an American invested in the system? How could this have happened *anyway*?

I didn't sleep for a week. I allowed myself to wallow in the shock, betrayal, fear and anxiety until I was utterly exhausted on every level. I felt terrible.

Finally, I just couldn't live there anymore. I couldn't bring myself to step into the "victim" role, when I know that there are no victims, no perpetrators – those labels are only illusion. That whole victim / perpetrator / enabler cycle – it's over. We are up to something much bigger now, and this is the season of my life to bring that understanding home.

So I began to get curious: *"Why has this event been handled to me now and what, if anything, am I to do about it, and how might my experience serve others?"*

My heart began to open ever wider as I thought about my fellow passengers on this journey to – *Where?*

I probed the Internet to find the other survivors. I say "survivors" because some had actually taken their lives already. I felt like I was having a "virtual Titanic" experience. I dreamed of all of those people strewn over the ocean's inky blackness, a few still safe in life boats, but the rest struggling in their tiny life-vests against the freezing and formidable current.

I felt isolated.

There was so little information to be found. It felt strange and disturbing to be going through something so deeply affecting to us all without being able to reach out to one another.

There is something almost mythical that happens in a shared crisis – a profound 'bonding experience" if you will – when human beings survive a significant test together they are forever joined in subtle and unsubtle ways. I literally *felt* these people, though I knew none of them.

I wondered if they were alright and what they were going through. How many were going to be affected by this financial tsunami and what were they feeling? I wondered how their lives had been irrevocably changed overnight, and what they were doing to cope with the change. I worried about their families and their charities. How were they managing or surviving? Would there be any relief for those who lost everything at an advanced age? I imagined 80 year-olds who were penniless with no family or visible means of support, some of them on medications or in institutions – what would they do? I imagined college educations that would never arrive for the young people. Were people hiding out in their new circumstances – ashamed, embarrassed, humiliated, afraid – depressed? How could we help one another, and how would that look? Perhaps a government program or a private foundation? Who were all these people who had been visited by this cold unseen iceberg in the night, and were they thinking my thoughts too? Would they even talk to a stranger at this crucial emotional time?

The Universe had my attention. This was a collective death, and as Neitchze wrote, "Death concentrates the mind." I was Awake and Vulnerable for perhaps the first time in a long time. I was imminently *receptive*.

Yet, I couldn't reconcile this paradox:

I had been living like a multi-millionaire for years, basing all of my financial decisions, my life choices and my plans on the belief that I was wholly secure and my future was assured ….. ***And the money was never there.***

The Madoff scheme had been operating for twenty-plus years … a complete and utter illusion.

What does that say about our ability to create with our minds?

Is it possible that what we need are ***better stories?***

For twenty years I had been living in a consciousness that said *there is enough*, I could achieve all my dreams, I was safe and whole and free …. I was perceived in a certain way, and even carried myself differently out of that confidence…I felt powerful, and at peace.

Now, the money is gone, but *I* am still here. I am still *me*.

So which is it? Does our life create our thought? …. Or does our thought create our life? And which choice has power in it?

I began to live in the question: ***Where then does my True Wealth abide?***

Every day I was more acutely aware that none of this "stuff" was me – not my money, nor my home, nor my clothes, my jaguar, my sassy red hair, my *identity*.

The truth is, we don't *own* anything. We don't even own our bodies … we are just tenants here, little columns of energy called by this name and that. When we start believing that we "own" things, it is *we* who are owned by them, enslaved by the fear of loss (death).

What if we woke up one day to realize that we existed completely independently of our material possessions and we no longer had any attachment to them? What if we did not identify with them *as us*, or as that which defines us? Suppose we saw them merely as shiny particles?

What if we woke up to discover that our souls are so magnificent, so expansive and eternal that we literally can not be bound by *any* limited concept of who we *think* we are? What if we are greater than all of the billions we could ever conjure? And what if we knew all this was true in the very core of our bones? *Could anything then harm us or touch us, or even kill us?*

It would be like swallowing the Sun!

You may call me an optimist, or naïve.

I do believe in Divine Perfection. I believe that life and all of its events have *purpose* and that those events come to us always and ultimately for our growth and higher good, nudging us into the fullest expression of our Self. After all, life always makes sense looking back. When all the dross has fallen away, we are fully and finally revealed as the figure in the stone that always abided there.

For some reason, my soul has called this in – this Madoff thing is far too big to be arbitrary.

After all …. This is a very august group of people – intelligent, talented and creative – these are people who have done things with their lives. They have contributed enormously to society, they have built hospital wings, university libraries, they have furthered important medical research, created scholarship programs, they have written books and made movies and art, they have helped to shape and carry the culture. What purpose is being served by *this* group of souls undergoing this challenge and transformation? Where is the *divine equity* in this situation?

I am reminded of a quote by John Kennedy when he was asked how he became a hero …. He replied, "*It was easy – they sunk my boat*".

I decided to mediate to see if I could find some answers. This message came:

> 'We live in a time of great change and turbulence….we need ways to re-align with our Higher selves, and to stabilize and balance ourselves…. everything is in Divine order….a win-win situation is building for all…you need to have blind faith that all is working for the highest outcome and good of all …. You need to be a model

of abundance. Embrace change … align it with your soul's purpose.

You are going to write a book about this. The process will pull the different parts of your life together and draw on your varied experience. This book will be important for many people, it is a message that is greatly needed right now.'

I heard my rebellious outer voice say, *but I am not a writer!*

And my inner voice said: 'Of course, it makes perfect sense'.

Bernie L. Madoff put a face on what may one day be seen as the total collapse of our financial systems and the thinking behind them that no longer serves us collectively. The complexity of our problems has outpaced our ability to solve them with historical approaches. We can no longer exist independently; we are a completely interdependent world.

Because we are all part of humanity, what happens to each of us must in some ways affect all others. Our experience is universal in nature, and it is speaking to humanity at this time.

What if this turns out to be a *Hero's Journey* for America? What if Bernie turns out to be the dragon in the road which forced the *test* that will lead us to profound renewal? What if he actually did us a favor by helping to expose the dark underbelly of greed, corruption and negligence that threatened our society and our country's future? Can we, *have we* set out on a road to transformation? Are we individually and collectively up to it? What if this is really birth masquerading as catastrophe? Once the hero commits and sets foot on the path, *all the rules change and the whole Universe conspires to assist him.* I do not have biological children, but what I know about birth is that it is painful when resisted – and, resistance is futile.

The Madoff phenomenon is an *archetype* for our time, a lens through which to shine a light, when so many everywhere are going through their own trauma of loss and grief, struggling to survive, to find their right livelihood and their life purpose, longing to find authentic ways of being while the world as we have known it is deconstructing and morphing into something altogether new and (hopefully) greater than we have known before.

I know this has to do with love, I am just not sure exactly how yet … something about giving and receiving love, creating space for greater and greater love, facilitating the flow of love to others – for individuals and groups, for countries….

When I asked in meditation what it is we most need for humanity right now, I heard two words:

> ***Reconnection*** …. Not "Connection", but "*Reconnection*" … meaning that where we need to be is already known to us on some level …. reconnection with ourselves, reconnection with each other, reconnection with our higher guides and intuition, reconnection with the things that nurture us and nurture others – like Mother Nature – reconnection with the Divine.

> ***Empty Spaces*** … a necessary emptying out, so that the new can come in to fill us up, fill our hearts, fill our lives with greater meaning, and fulfill our desires and Purpose.

When IT asked what I wanted to create, I answered:

> '*I want to create a space of Connection/Community/Healing & Wholeness, which will allow and facilitate individuals and groups to transform their fear of change into*

42

positive manifestations ... .aligned with their individual gifts and higher purpose'

These days I am thinking less about how I will *survive*, and more about how I will *contribute* – trusting I will somehow be supported in the balance.

Once I was able to move out of the fear, (and it was intense, I do not wish to minimize it for any of us) I was able to see the **Gifts of Devastation**. I began to acknowledge and bless the changes arriving softly as a result of this experience. I began to practice Gratitude.

There have been so many gifts and shifts in my being:

I am more vulnerable: I no longer have an illusory layer of protection between myself and others…my walls are down.

I am more accessible: new people and possibilities are beginning to show up that might never have arrived while I was in my ivory tower. (Who knows, perhaps there is a partner on the way!)

My relationship with my family has deepened as I experienced more empathy and more connection; in my vulnerability, they stepped in to help me and invest their love in me.

I am open to new possibilities: I had my life planned out within the confines of what I had accumulated, but my design did not include the infinite creativity of the Universe, or help from anybody else! How small was my thinking! God laughed at my tiny plan.

I am learning to ask for help: As the daughter of an Air Force colonel, I was raised to be self-reliant. I preferred to be the one leading, providing, teaching, contributing (*in control*). Now I am able to allow others to contribute their gifts to me! I am able to *receive* more every day – what a Blessing this has been!

I am experiencing a new humility: I watched my pride erupt as I pleaded with my attorney to take my case on contingency, and returned the clothes I had bought before Christmas to the department stores. I am letting go of false pride. I am clarifying and cleansing the patterns that no longer serve me.

I now experience and accept feelings: I used to beat myself up for not being perfect, and I felt guilty when I was afraid, depressed or angry – in other words, when I was human! What I see now is that in order to live a fulfilled life, or even to write this book, I must go through the fear. How can I be empathetic or understand the fears of others without experiencing them myself? I am right where I am supposed to be, feeling my feelings out loud so that I and others can see and hear something valuable. This fear is purposeful. This fear is teaching me. This fear is calling me to *non-fear*.

My heart is expanding as I am thinking about all the people who face this reality every day of their lives, not just the Madoff survivors but all of the extraordinary people who are working three jobs to pay the bills, or have no job, or are too ill to work.

And as my heart expands, I feel more connected to my fellow human beings, to guidance, and to all the infinite and creative possibilities in the Universe.

I am letting go and simplifying. I am finding the *true value* in my life and pruning away unnecessary objects, beliefs, relationships. I am getting Lighter!

At the same time, I am experiencing greater clarity.

I am being called to expand my focus and train it on my true desires, and the direction my heart is calling for – otherwise how will it manifest? I heard once that God only enters into equal partnerships. *I am learning to partner with the Universe.*

I am moving from fear and contraction to faith and action! I have a new sense of freedom, I somehow know that my future *is* assured, and I am open to it being more wonderful than my mind can invent.

I am grateful every day for all the small and large Blessings in my life!

I am being called to Radical Trust in the face of evidence that would call me to fear – in other words, I am being asked to consciously *live what is real,* versus the illusions we are bombarded with every day. *I am being called to trust in myself, in the hidden hands, and a future that I cannot see yet,* **but sense**.

It isn't always easy to find the Gift when we are in the pain of letting go, or when the fear threatens to overwhelm us, when the barbarians are at the gate. Yet everyone I have ever heard speak about surviving a significant trial or illness or loss in their life, has said it was the "greatest teacher they ever had" and one of "the best things that ever happened" to them.

A wise teacher in India once posed the question to me**, "*What does a man have when he has lost everything?"*

"Freedom", he said.

And from that place, we can create Everything.

From Utter Despair To A Hope For A Brighter Future
Robert Halio

My name is Robert Halio. Up until Dec. 11th, 2008, I was happily retired and living a life of leisure in Boca Raton, Florida. I had sold my small business in 2005 and felt secure about my future as my wife and I had always saved our money, and we had been invested with Bernie Madoff for about twenty something years. On Dec. 11th, I received a phone call from my son, who works in finance, that Madoff had turned himself in, claiming that the whole business had been a Ponzi scheme and that there was no money left. I almost fell to the floor. I couldn't catch my breath and thought that I might be having a heart attack. I was in total shock. How could this happen to us? It must be a bad dream! My brain couldn't process the news.

My wife and I had worked and planned and saved for 40 years to finally retire and feel that we had no worries for the rest of our lives. We would be able to take care of ourselves. We had cashed in our life insurance policies years ago to give the money to Madoff. We had no long term health care because we felt that we had enough of our own money to self insure. The earth had opened up and swallowed us. The fear was overpowering and it was difficult

46

to even think straight. There were so many problems. Where do we start?

We lost 95% of our money to Madoff. We knew that our lives as we had known them were over. We lost our fancy cars, our home in the Hamptons, our credit and lived like church mice in a dark, hot house. We were afraid to breathe. We sold everything that we could monetize. Our home was protected by the Homestead Act in Florida, but could we afford to keep it?

We cried daily and shook with fear. We tried to find any kind of work, but could find nothing. I tried to find work as a schoolteacher, took a test, but there were no jobs. I tried for the post office, took a test, same result. I tried every retail store in Boca Raton, but no one was hiring.

We were getting more and more desperate. My wife went to real estate school, spending some dearly needed dollars, but we felt that would be the best chance for her to make some money. Her timing could not have been worse. She has spent far more money on schooling, advertising and real estate fees than she has made. She works really hard, puts in lots of time but alas, there are no sales. She has earned only a tiny bit of money compared to what her bills have been. We didn't know that it was so costly to be a real estate agent.

I could not find any work in my field, which was process serving, a pretty specialized business. I could not open my own business as I had no capital with which to fund a new business. My wife and I agreed that we wanted to stay in our home as long as we could afford to do so. So we gave up any shopping, entertainment and restaurants, everything that cost money and just tried to pay our bills for our home.

I decided to drive people to the airports, to doctors, wherever. I also mailed flyers offering house watching services. We got one job house watching. It didn't even cover the cost of printing the flyer.

But we were determined to survive, no matter what we had to do. We had been extremely philanthropic people, always believing that we were fortunate in our lives and it was our honor to give to so many charities. That stopped dead.

I carried a lot of shame. We had fallen from on high to the very bottom, through no fault of our own, but nevertheless, we were ashamed to a certain extent. It was very hard to face our friends and our community in general, knowing that we could no longer socialize with them for the most part. We have wonderful, supportive and kind friends and they made us feel as comfortable as possible with our new status. Status had never mattered to us. We always considered ourselves to be low key and quiet about our lives. We appreciated every luxury that we enjoyed in our "former" lives. We use that expression a lot, "former" lives.

I can't say that I was not embarrassed to be driving people all around. Most people have been very nice and supportive of our efforts. It makes me feel so good, knowing that people are happy with our service and really like us so much. We have established many very warm relationships with our clients. One recommends another and that's how our business has grown. We will never live close to the way that we once did, but this new business takes some of the pressure off in terms of fearing that we will lose our home.

I have learned that material things don't matter. I shop in my closet as my wife does in hers. We don't miss the fancy cars. Transportation is just that, transportation. Expensive dinners are totally unimportant and we don't miss them at all. We cannot travel, but we have lots of great memories of trips that we have taken in the past We don't go to theatre or shows. Those would be lots of fun for us, but we choose to save the money for a bit of a cushion. We watch a lot of TV and eat lots of pizza.

Sometimes it's hard when we hear friends talking about shopping, traveling, restaurants, shows, etc., but we have to get used to it and all of those things are so transient, that once they are over, it's almost as if they never happened. They become memories, just like the ones that we already have. I don't think we need to add any more memories. We have enough of them to keep for the rest of our lives.

It is most important to keep one's health. Sometimes I felt as if that was going to be a tough job considering the stress that we have been undergoing. But so far, so good. I had felt very depressed for many, many months. It was hard to accept such losses. I felt that I had lost my identity, along with my self-respect. People judge you by what material things you have in your possession, your lifestyle, your money, and that is how they determine your status in the world. I felt crushed and anonymous, as if I had become transparent, and just didn't count anymore.

I was a person who was pitied. And there just might be some Schadenfreude somewhere along the way. It's taken a year to restore my confidence in myself as a provider and as a man. I'm doing the best that I can under the circumstances. I cannot start over in any career. I don't have the money or the strength to do so.

But I am happy with the progress that we have made in our business and look forward to increasing it each year. My wife and I can't go on forever driving and lugging suitcases, but we will do the best that we can and that's all we can do.

I gave up my golf membership but I still play tennis in between driving and I have lots of fun doing that. Besides, it's also a physical outlet for the stress that I feel. My wife and I are lucky to be able to support each other. When one feels a little anxious, the other one can be very supportive and ally any fears. We've been through hell and we're still here. We are fighters and we will not give up. Bernie Madoff and his family of crooks and thugs will not destroy us. We will survive.

What Remains
Jeannene Langford

I still remember getting the phone call that would color my life in so many ways. On December 12th, 2008, the manager of the partnership where I had put a large portion of my life's savings called and said we were invested in Madoff Securities and all of our money was gone. At first I thought he was kidding. It became clear that he was serious and immediately I fell apart.

I had not come from money and I worked for 30 years as a design professional, the last 17 years as a single parent. My lost money also was income from a house I had sold at the top of the market in 2006. Since the real estate market was too shaky and it wasn't time for me to buy another house I looked for a safe place that was liquid and diversified to invest my money. I turned to a friend who was a self made millionaire and who I knew to be very smart about investing. He was willing to help me out by giving me access to a partnership he had started years ago. I was convinced that his strategy was stable and safe. I never knew it was Madoff we were investing in. In 2006 I started putting money into the account earning between 4 and 8 percent interest, or so I thought.

The news about Madoff revealed $65 billion was lost in the Ponzi scheme, a number that was hard to wrap my head around. Then as more of the story came out we learned of the SEC's neglect and complicity. In January 2009 I found out because I was in a feeder fund I would not be eligible for SIPC insurance. At that point I lost faith in my government's ability to serve and protect investors..

My life felt so surreal. I've heard when a person dies that their life flashes before their eyes, and while I was not dying it felt like a big part of me just had. What flashed in front of my eyes was the past – all the years I had spent working to get ahead in my career, the nights I brought my daughter to the office with me or had the sitter feed her dinner, read her a story and tuck her in bed. All the time I spent working to get ahead and get a nest egg tucked away for the future seemed so pointless now.

Next my thoughts moved to the future; my savings also represented the foundation for a new life. I had spent the past 9 months working with a partner flushing through the details of getting a new business ready to launch. It was a big step away from the corporate work I had done for years and was so burnt out on. Finally, I was establishing a business I could really own and grow. In part we were going to self-fund the company and I was to live on savings until the business made a profit. I was also planning to buy a condo so my daughter who was finishing up at school could move back in with me and finish her program.

How am I going to survive this? I had no plan for being 54, single and broke. I had been carefully saving all my life and took calculated risks with my money. Could I even afford the one bedroom apartment I was in? It was hard to determine how to budget and plan what to do next. The sense of having no control at all was psychologically distressing. When you over think, you can cut yourself off from the wisdom of your emotions, which are much better at assessing actual preferences. You lose the ability to know what you really want. Thinking I had little time to lose multiplied the pressure to get to work quickly and rebuild.

Then I thought of my friends who were also involved with Madoff. We were all hurting. I joined the Madoff survivors group on line and heard so many more difficult stories of people who were in a similar of worse situation than I was. It was heartbreaking. Shock, disbelief, and despair dominated my thoughts. Many close friends wanted to help and a few key ones knew how.

Through all the rubble I found a few precious gems. The first was understanding how much I meant to family and friends and really feeling love and compassion just for being myself. It opened the gateway to realizing how rich I was with people who loved me.

The next gem was much harder; it was about learning how to receive. My father always encouraged me to be self sufficient no matter what. Now, I had no choice but to accept the help that was being offered. My friends helped with emotional support, groceries, professional services, rent and more. My daughter whom I had been supporting through her schooling set a new plan to get a job taking on much more of her own personal financial responsibility.

Moving out of despair and grief was slow but acceptance came in waves. I was able to stay "in the moment" more of the time, which allowed me to connect with a stronger more centered part of myself. This is where 25 years of Buddhist practice came in handy. My acts and feeling of desperation turned to a pragmatic approach for carving out a future, and rebuilding my life. I knew it was not going to be an easy task due to double-digit unemployment and my age. Nevertheless being with what is and moving was the answer.

One of the ways I maintained mental and physical strength was through cycling. It is always important to give back. I now was going to have to curtail donating time or money to causes I believed in. I did not want that happen. I found a charity century bike ride that I could participate in, the Best Buddies Charity which helps intellectually disabled kids get socialized and lead more full lives. I remember saying "Screw you Bernie, I can still give back."

Together through friends and family we raised over $1500. I finished the ride with a renewed belief in myself and other people.

It's taken awhile to sort out what money really meant to me, moving through the roles of victim and beginning to fight back. In early December 2009 (about one year after "the phone call") I was contacted to testify at the hearings before the House Finance Services Committee in Washington, DC regarding the Madoff scandal. The process of reliving the experience one more time and taking action to fight back was not only personally cathartic but helped give face to investors who need and deserve help from the government. What I was able to offer was the perspective of a feeder fund investor that was not rich, not Jewish, and did not live on the East coast. I was one of the over 11,000 victims not allowed to make an individual SIPC claim based on the antiquated definition of "customer". I flew to Washington, DC and I was one of five investors who testified before Congress. What I experienced was many people working with many different agendas working to resolve the settlements to their own best advantage. I maintain that what needs to happen is ALL who were victims of the Madoff Ponzi scheme need to be treated fairly and protected by the governing body that not only sanctioned this business but encouraged it's growth.

"The past is the past and what remains important is the action I take today" is the mantra I put in front of myself every morning. It does not negate what happened and it does not mean I won't fight to resolve what I can with SIPC. I have this opportunity today to appreciate the abundant blessings in life, strive to be the best I can be and move on.

From Innocent Sunny Oaks, To The Biggest Ponzi Scheme In The World
SM

My mom in 1922 and my dad in 1917 were both born into poverty. Both of their mothers' were Russian immigrants entering the U.S. through Ellis Island at the turn of the 20th century; my mother's father was Polish. My dad's father was born in what is now Chinatown in New York City but it is believed his family immigrated from Germany. They were poor immigrants like so many others coming to America for a better life.

My dad is now 92. He is blind and deaf. He always worked very hard. Born totally blind in one eye with a diminutive physique, he always had a serious analytical personality. He graduated high school at 16, from New York University at 18 and entered medical school as the youngest student in the class.

My mom, now 88 was a clever child. She became independent at the age of 13 as her family could not afford to keep her. She lived with several different unofficial "foster" families until she graduated high school. First she lived with a pharmacist, then a teacher, and finally a baker. At intervals she would stay with her maternal grandparents. She always had endless spirit and energy. I always wonder what she could have been given different circumstances and a different generation. With the encouragement of an aunt, she went to a nursing school on a stipend of $18 a month paid to her by the hospital.

They met in 1940, two opposites, the serious med student and carefree nursing student. They were married at Sunny Oaks in the Catskill Mountains in Woodridge, New York, September 1942. Sunny Oaks was small group of summer bungalows owned by my mother's grandfather and step-grandmother. It was the same place my mom would take refuge between her foster experiences.

My parents moved to Florida from New York in the early 1950's. I was the fourth child born in the mid 1950's in a small segregated rural town on the East coast of Florida. Our house held five kids, two dogs and any injured or orphaned animals anyone came across; it was about 1200 square feet. We lived surrounded by tomato fields, went barefoot, never worried about clothes matching – we had food and shelter. I had the safety of three sisters with me in our tiny bedroom crowed with sets of bunk beds. Dad was the only MD in town, Mom was his nurse. Practicing medicine was about healing and helping never about money. I remember Dad bringing home a sack of potatoes, a sweet potato pie, a cup and saucer. He did free physicals for kids, umpired little league games. Childhood was wonderful: unpretentious, unencumbered, and easy.

Summers were the best. When I was young we would go to New York sometimes, a seemingly foreign land coming from the rural south. I was awestruck seeing "apartments", milk sold in machines, trains underground and basements! The tap water seemed different, the air smelled different, people were different.

We would go see our grandmother, great aunts and uncles, cousins at Sunny Oaks. My mother was very close to her mother, but much of her inspiration and encouragement and support came from her aunts, her mother's half sisters. As beautiful, smart, talented and loving my grandmother was, my mom's guidance and role models were her aunts.

I fell in love in 1972 at the age of 18 with a surfer hitch hiker. That began a new adventure turning away from academics and college to an education in life. I joined him on a tug boat and traveled to places like Nicaragua and Dominica living in a box on deck the size of a coffin or living in a tuberculosis quarantine hut. Ultimately I went back to school but left again to live on the tug with him in Cayenne, French Guiana; it was a lovely small homemade rustic boat. My mantra was live simply, the theme I had learned from my parents. I loved, I trusted; I was naive. I also had no clue our first baby was due in six months.

My soon-to-be husband and I left the tug boat and moved back to Florida. We lived week to week. Neither of us had finished college. With the help of student work study program, a job changing tires, and a small mobile home my husband finished college. We had our second child by graduation but he lucked out getting a job in the timber industry in Georgia. We continued to live simply, love and trust.

We moved back to a small Florida beach town in 1982. My husband went back to working on a boat and I took care of our two young children. Life was pay check to pay check. We rented a house and had very few possessions. An old car, cloth diapers, no washer or dryer. Life was in the slow lane.

In the mid 1980s we left the boating world. My husband began his own business, a lawn service. He hooked up a trailer to the back of our 1963 Rambler and started knocking on doors. We didn't know we were poor. It never crossed our minds. We were healthy and happy, we continued to live simply, love and trust.

Around the time our third child was on the way in the late 1980s my mom began talking about an investment that paid a set percent. Her aunts from Sunny Oaks told her about it and encouraged her to invest. They made 20% on their money and returns were steady. My parents did not invest immediately. My aunts loved my mom and they thought it would be a wise investment for my parents. When they finally decided to invest it turned out to be with the accountants and feeder to Madoff, Avellino & Bienes; my folks were guaranteed 18% a year.

It all seemed to check out, so they in turn told us, their five children to invest. My husband and I had $5,000 saved. It was everything we had. I had tried traditional brokers, Merrill Lynch and Prudential, but I didn't have enough money for their minimum, and no one was really interested in me as a client. I saw rich friends getting in on deals with their brokers but not me. I finally thought Avellino &

Biennes would be it! So, I invested my $5,000 in A&B in the late 1980s.

In 1992 I received a letter from A&B saying they were closing and they were returning my money (which included the accrued profits totaling about $7,500.00). They explained they were investigated by the SEC, found of no wrong doing but fined for some registration/bookkeeping errors. I was really disappointed about their closing. I clearly remember the SEC's comments regarding the situation and discussing it with my parents.

Right after A&B closed, my mom's phone rang. It was Bernard Madoff. Then my brother's phone rang. It was Bernard Madoff. He was soliciting their business. He did not call me or my sisters and invite us to invest. My mom spoke to Annette Bongiorno, Madoff's secretary, after her account was set up and a few months later Annette suggested we create a partnership. So we did. We opened our partnership account, four sisters with $20,000 each or $80,000 total. It was again all we had. Our oldest sister and her husband were the keepers of the account.

This $20,000 represented our total life savings. Having three kids was getting progressively more expensive, but I knew I had this account and I would let my money grow. In my mind it represented the future and I hoped with my sisters and parents we could each withdraw the small profit it would make for some income when we were seniors. This income would mean food, shelter, medical care, living expenses. There would be no glamour.

I paid no attention to the Madoff account. I received year-end tax information from my sister, but otherwise she tracked the account, kept all the records etc. Three kids were consuming me, and my sister and her husband were smart. It was the perfect set-up for a simpleton like me.

In 2004, we decided to divide our partnership into individual accounts. It only made sense. Some sisters wanted to invest more

57

money and I knew I couldn't add to my account and would eventually need to withdraw money to pay taxes. Without problems or questions, our partnership was dissolved and we each had our own individual direct account. I was now alone getting my first BLMIS documents. Ironically, my beloved sister who kept our Madoff records for years died in 2005.

There was never any thought or concern about Madoff. I knew he had been checked out by the SEC and I was a client. I knew puts and calls were balanced against stock purchases. My returns were steady, but not outstanding. Sometimes I made money on puts and calls, sometimes on stocks, but in the end it balanced out. Our small account was our safety net, our future.

<u>December 11, 2008</u>

My Mom received a phone call from a niece: "Aunt, do you have an account with Bernie Madoff?"

"Yes," replied my mom.

"He was arrested today". Fatefully, I was visiting them that day. I stayed calm not wanting to upset my parents, but inside felt a sickening surreal feeling. I knew I had no money at that moment. My future life flashed before my eyes. I called my brother and sisters – in all we had six accounts. All of my money was gone, as well as the majority of my siblings' money and large part of my parents'.

In some ways, life didn't change at all after Dec 11, 2008; in another way it totally changed. I still had my wonderful husband, children, grandchildren and family. We had one child in college, but the costs were primarily covered through scholarships and grants although she did give up her apartment and move back home. I knew we had SIPC coverage which was a relief; I even called the SIPC office to confirm the coverage and the terms of the insurance. I was assured I had coverage of up to $500,000 in securities and $100,000 in cash. This was far exceeding the value of my account so I thought I would be made whole once the paper work was done. I confirmed and reconfirmed my calculations with SIPC. Between Dec 8 and Feb 19, 2009, I cycled through my feelings and had come to a comfortable space. Until Feb 20th, 2009, when the trustee and his attorney announced at a meeting they were defining net equity as cash in – cash out. This was devastating as it contradicted what SIPC had told me over the previous months, it changed the terms of the coverage and left me with possibility of recovering only 14 cents on the dollar.

My first reaction was to conserve everything but I soon realized I was already doing that; I never wasted food anyway, I shut off lights, kept the house temperature on the edge of too hot in the summer, I heated the house with wood in the winter, had a garden, drove an old small car and bought clothes second hand at yard sales and thrift stores. This was already my life--simple and frugal, but now with no safety net again as in our youth and no prospect of recovering our savings.

I began sitting in the dark, boiling bones for soups, bathing quickly, and hanging out all wash. Every garbage pile I passed on the side of the road we eyed. When our college daughter began bringing her friends' leftovers home I realized I needed to find a new way to face my life and the situation. I realized I was paralyzed and spiraling down.

Wounded emotions and falling into the abyss

It is a strange feeling to have been a victim of Madoff. My emotions range from feeling violated to anger to depression to disbelief. The loss of my savings was like a death of what my future life should have been as I age. It is the loss of my sense of security. I had wanted to lead an independent and modest senior life with my husband. I am innocent of any wrongdoing but felt the world has blamed me. I am called greedy and stupid for using Madoff as my brokerage firm. I don't understand why victims were being blamed.

59

I became paralyzed and withdrawn; to this day we have not told most friends and some family this has happened to us. To this day I feel a sense of shame.

As time has passed, I have tried to understand how my family became connected to Madoff. I have since discovered I am a third generation investor and now know, Mrs. Ruth Madoff's parents, the Alperns were dear friends with my mom, my mom's aunts and uncles that frequented Sunny Oaks in the summers, I probably met the Alperns as a child.

I don't fit the public image of Madoff direct investors. We are a lower income family that now, with the tax relief given the victims, will not get taxes back but qualify for earned income credit as a refund. As far as I can tell, my husband and I are or were the poorest direct investors of Mr. Madoff's. I knew nothing about Madoff's exclusivity, minimum investment or allure. This has been a shock to me. I had no clue.

There has been a great injustice by mischaracterization of the investors. I am proof. There are no vacations, clubs, pools, fine wines, and jewels in my life – none of the amenities the press seems to assign to the Madoff direct investors. I have dirty fingernails, calloused feet and uncut, undyed hair. I have never had a manicure or pedicure, and now for sure never will. My last job was as a maid. Going to the doctor or dentist is on an as needed basis and it's not for a cleaning or check up.

Stories like mine have been avoided by the media. It is much more sensational for the public to believe Madoff investors were all rich or famous and because of their greed they are getting their due. This false portrayal lets the average person feel good, laugh and think it will never happen to them. But I am them, that's the secret.

I don't feel sorry for myself, for living this kind of life. But what I am angry about is this kind of life was my choice and that any choice has been taken away. I would have done things differently

60

from the age of 34 to 54 years of age to secure my future ability to live independently.

I am heartbroken that I will have to depend on you, the public, for my survival as a senior. The future holds a life of welfare, federal assistance and Medicaid.

Probably the hardest part of this travesty is hearing the stories about other innocent people and their emotional and financial struggles, particularly the elderly and those that committed suicide. I can't fathom a group of human beings, Madoff, Frank DiPascali and all others involved yet to be named could do this to anyone . To have the want and need for greed, to feel power at the hurt of others is unconscionable. Their arrogance is a sickness that has become all too common in American culture.

Healing

There is no healing from an experience like this. Like a chronic disease, I have learned to live with it, take medication when necessary; some days are better than others. I am trying to be more philosophical and reflective about my life. I live each day as I face it and work at letting go of thoughts about my future, letting go of my anger. I have lost trust in Wall Street, the Securities and Exchange Commission, our government and in people in general. I feel like I have had an awakening to unsavory parts of American life and culture: corruption, greed, power, arrogance. I feel small, powerless and discounted, but enlightened to these things. The SEC will say *mea culpa*, Madoff is in a country club jail, his family will live happily ever after, the trustee for SIPC will earn more by paying us less and the Madoff investors will have years of court battles. My greatest solace has come from other victims, people I don't know, have never seen, but I now love and cherish like family. I have found understanding, camaraderie and support. I have gathered my inner strength thanks to them, and found my resolve.

Years ago a Catholic priest told me "no great philosopher has ever equated spiritual maturity with material possessions". I am clutching his words closely and reminded daily I am defined by who I am as a human being; kind, loving and so much more. I am working on finding peace and moving forward with my personal growth. It doesn't mean I don't wonder what my future will hold and remove the fears that haunt me at night. My situation of being caught in this web of deceit and lies hasn't changed, but how I am handling it has. In the end, I will live and die like every one else. What happens in between will be forever changed. I am still trying to figure it out.

Elisabetta Sandolo

I am a Madoff investor. I began my life in Western Europe and came to America as an immigrant child with my family in the early 1970's. We had relatives that had come to America in the 50's and 60's, we were the last to come over. My parents, just like their siblings, began as small business owners and managed to put aside enough money to send us all to college. They paid for my room and board and a third of my first two years of college; the rest was paid for by grants, loans and my on-campus job. My parents worked long hours for as long as I could remember. My mom started working at the age of five selling her father's catch of the day in the streets. I vowed to pay my way through college as soon as possible as my "gift" back to my mom and dad. In my third year, I began my co-op program. For the next three years, I worked for one semester, saved up most of the money, then went to school for a semester. I earned my bachelor's degree in my fifth year.

In 1992, I had just begun my second full-time job and that's when my folks got their check back from Avellino & Bienes, a feeder fund into Madoff. They had begun investing in 1990 so they were just getting their feet wet with investing in the market. They didn't know anything about Bernie Madoff; my mom's cousin had been investing with Madoff for years.

About a year after they received their money back with one year's interest, they were advised to pool money together with other small investor/family members and form a partnership. My mom, uncle and the other family members asked me to manage the partnership since I had always been good with numbers.

Although I had always planned on starting my own business and really wanted to do it by myself, I agreed to be the managing partner of the family partnership as a side job and favor to my

63

mom. That was January of 1993. We opened our account with Madoff by going to one of his feeder representative's office and getting on a conference call with Bernard Madoff. The feeder rep had previously discussed everything on the phone with my mom and uncle and he felt that between five initial people we didn't have enough money to make it worth his while to add us to his partnership. He suggested we could form our own partnership and he would get Bernie to take us on as a direct account.

My mom and uncle were excited. I was not. I wanted to make it on my own with no complications of family involvement. I had seen my parents go through some tough times with relatives who had promised things in exchange for helping them but never delivered on their promises. After seeing my parents get hurt my view was to make it on your own and never depend on anyone to get to where you want to be financially.

At the feeder rep's office, we were shown the press release that the SEC had made clearing Madoff as a custodian. That same day that we spoke to Madoff for the first and last time on the phone, we signed the account opening agreement and left a check made out to BLMIS for the very first time. Our initial investment was $50,000. The feeder got the account agreement and check to Madoff where we were assigned Annette Bongiorno as our contact at Madoff.

We began with five people and I contributed $10,000 at first, half of what I had saved at the time. I knew my family's savings would be invested, so at that time I also decided that it was best for me to only make minimal contributions in future years and keep the rest of my money separate "just in case" the investment didn't do as well as it had historically. I always thought that if my folks and other relatives invested all their savings with Madoff and something went wrong, I could help them out with my savings and alternate investments! I would save them if they needed saving! It was early on. I had no experience with Madoff investments at that point. I had no need for him and his firm. I was an entrepreneur!

For the next 10 years, I began and ran a very successful contract employment agency. I had very dedicated managers in large corporations that often felt they were better off hiring from a small agency they trusted rather than a large one with a lot of ineffective talking heads. These key contacts helped the business thrive. I always re-invested all of the profits back into the business. It not only helped grow the business but it also kept everyone paid on-time without worrying about clients paying their bills and without relying on outside sources for funding such as loans from banks. This reinvesting in the business also kept most of my hard earned money out of Madoff since I'd always believed no investment was 100% secure.

In 2004, my mother had become incapacitated with a serious illness. She had always been there for me and now found herself alone, infirm and outside of the U.S.A. where all of her family resided. At this point, I had two options: hire a full-time, live-in nurse for her or take care of her myself. I thought long and hard on it and finally made a tough decision. She deserved a family member to be there for her.

I sold all of my corporate contracts to an international placement agency, closed down shop and sent all of the money to Madoff. My retirement money would be safe there. Madoff was good as gold to me at that point. He'd proven himself to me time and time again in the past 10 plus years!

Although I had been successful in my own business, I hadn't been as successful as Madoff. I had always taken on much more risk as a small business owner than I would be taking by having such a successful money manager just grow my retirement fund now. I had been working 80 hours a week for years up until about 2003. It was 2004 and I was still tired from all of that work. During those five busy years from 1998 to 2003, I had a responsibility to my employees to keep them all working. I had a responsibility to my investors, to keep their investment working and earning. I had a responsibility to my family, to help them as needed. In the meantime, I had already been a money manager for my handicapped brother for the past ten years. All of this experience and hard work, combined with my mother's sudden illness, solidified my choice to become the family caretaker and financial planner full time. I could afford to do this. I worked for twenty years, to save up for this day. The day had come.

Madoff had been investing our money now for over 10 years, we made between 8 and 12 percent a year. My uncle often pushed me to contact Madoff and ask if there was a way to make even higher returns. He thought, "if he can do those steady returns, maybe he has something even more profitable that we can invest in". As the partnership manager, I simply refused. We had formed the group because we wanted a safe and steady investment. We wanted to protect the money we had all worked decades to set aside for a rainy day and for later in life when we really needed it. The higher returns would mean more risk and I was not about to get my friends and relatives into a high risk investment situation. I wasn't greedy, I just wanted to build a retirement portfolio and not have to worry about going broke or losing a big chunk of money because some wild eyed, bushy tailed investment advisor got greedy.

My mother always supported my decisions. She knew that chasing riches and greed was not what we were all about. We kept true to our nature and to our family's values as a foundation. We were all about taking care of everyone and not about trying to get rich. That's why we came to America in the first place, so we could all be safe and secure and live well, not to get rich.

December 11, 2008, I wake up and get on the Internet. I was at the family home in Europe, which we have a mortgage on, by the way. I check email and my best friend had written, "Can you believe this psycho Madoff", with a link to a story on the web. "I hope your family's investment club didn't have any money with this guy."

My heart sank. My world just ended.

Everything I had worked for in the past 20 years was gone. Remember, I thought he was better off managing my money too since his track record in 20 years was better and more fluid than mine. I didn't trust myself managing all of the money. After all, I wasn't a super investor; I was a formerly successful small business owner. This didn't exactly qualify me to choose investments for over $4 million dollars and fifteen people.

I'll always remember my mom's stories about how she began at the age of five selling her father's freshly caught fish in the streets. She sold to folks who always tried to cheat her by short-changing her. She never let them get away with ripping her off and she was proud of that. She had never been swindled out of large sums... until Bernie came along. She feels like good-ole Bernie betrayed her like no one could ever do for seventy years!

I know many folks may take pleasure in what happened to my family and I and what I'm about to say but I don't care. Bernie was not my first scam. I have been swindled out of small amounts of money and things throughout my life. Mostly by non-immediate family, friends and business associates. I didn't do anything extraordinary and I don't want and never wanted sympathy for any reason or any situation I was in.

Any of my friends will tell you to whom they would go to first if they needed an emergency loan. It was myself. I was generous with loans and they would often turn into gifts. But I never really cared too much when this happened. Of course I'd have the normal reaction of anger, even rage. I don't like being taken for a chump. Eventually though, I'd always come to see it as a small price to pay to find out who you can and cannot trust. This was my philosophy and it still continues to be. I'm neither talking peanuts nor am I talking about large sums of money... until Bernie came along!

So how am I going forward and getting back on my feet? I'm still vowing to take care of my sick mother personally, but I must also work and rebuild. I am once again working in my former field of expertise for the next couple of years, re-building my professional relationships and starting all over again with a new small business. Yes, it's not all peachy keen and I can't start my new business today. Right now, I work pretty much every day of the week, on most weekends and pay my bills. I will soon be able to slowly set aside some money in the next year so I can take another stab at re-becoming a successful American entrepreneur! I learned in my past life as an entrepreneur is that success is easy to come by if you are honest and hard-working. People love honest, hard-working people with good ideas here in America. That's what this country is all about and I am all about that!

I have to admit; some days I don't think it will happen. I feel exhausted, used, abused and tossed to the curb by Madoff. Then I think about it and I realize that the only thing standing between me and my success is not Madoff, it's me. I won't let anyone stand between me and my success. Just as in the past, my future success is not measured by the amount of money I earn or save. It was never about that for me. It's about taking care of family and friends and even acquaintances and strangers that need my help. It's about taking care of and being there for the people that I love and care about. It's about taking care of people I don't even know. What else do we have to do with our lives? Is there something more important, more pressing? After paying the bills, no there isn't!

That's what I believe in and I will do it.

An American Success Story – Stolen by Madoff
Allan Goldstein

Andy Warhol said "Every one has fifteen minutes of fame." Here I was, Allan Goldstein, from 1342 East 18th Street in Brooklyn, going to appear before the Congress of the United States. Wow.

How did I get here? That's another story. I grew up on 1342 East 18th Street, a microcosm of lower middle class Jews before and after the Second World War. Every one had a steady job, just a job, no entrepreneurs. A six stories tall building with an elevator that worked most of the time and six apartments on every floor. Each floor at dinner time was filled with the smell of six apartments cooking dinner. If I remember, all was homogeneous and neighborly.

I graduated from James Madison High School in Brooklyn, and attended N.Y.U. I worked two different jobs to pay for my tuition, books and to have some spending money.

My mother always asked me what was I studying; expecting a doctor, a lawyer or an accountant. I didn't know what I wanted, so I became a business major. I really believe she thought I was a graduated CPA.

After college I was drafted into the army during the Korean War. While in Korea I saw action, was injured and received a Purple Heart. After completing my tour of duty I retuned home to Brooklyn. A few months later I went on a blind date and met my wife Ruth. We married in May of 1956 and we are still going strong after 53 fabulous years. What a great life we've had. We did it all.

I had a job earning $200 a month with a textile company. Ruth and I moved into a furnished basement apartment. We loved it. In September 1957, along came my daughter Bette. Soon after I was offered a job for $125 a week and thought I hit the lottery. I was working my way up the corporate ladder. We didn't have to go to our parents to eat anymore. Our second child, Alice was born in 1960

From that job came the next job for $300 a week. We were on the way. We bought a house and our son Larry was born in 1964. We were a family in a home filled with happiness and love.

We took a vacation for the first time, and started going out more often. I was running the out of town sales department for Crown Fabrics and was doing very well. A business associate asked me to go into business with him, with a minimum investment. I had always wanted to have my own business so I decided to take the risk. I joined him and in about one week realized I had made a mistake; I could not get along with the other partner. After six moths I left. Life was too short to go to work unhappy everyday.

I formed a new textile business with 4 other partners, Quorum Industries. It was very successful. We were a knitting mill and had our own plants in North Carolina. I took the company public; the world was my oyster.

Unfortunately, the textile industry and the fashion industry are very fickle. After ten very successful years I saw the hand writing on the wall and sold my interest in Quorum to my partners. I was left with a comfortable amount of money. I had plenty of time on my hands and bought a piece of land in Remsenburg, Long Island. The land was on a point with water on all sides. I became a contractor and built the house myself. I loved the home and I was very proud of the accomplishment.

Eventually, the Hamptons became too crowded. My wife and I decided that we needed a little more serenity in our lives. We sold the house and bought our dream house in Spencertown, New York, in Columbia County, right on the border of Western Massachusetts. No one in the world could have been happier living in a house as I was living in Spencertown. I love to fly fish. We had a forty acre lake on the property. I bought a 12 foot bass boat and would fish almost every evening, weather permitting.

My great passion is cooking and I consider myself a good chef. We entertained at home, having dinner parties two or three times a month. Everyone in the community sought after an invitation to our home for dinner. We had such a wonderful life and were loved by our community.

I always felt it was important to give back. One of my great pleasures was my charitable giving and helping out people who were less fortunate. I often donated dinners at my home to various charities. Those nights were truly special.

For many years I had all my investments with Merrill Lynch. I was getting a nice return on my money and was able to retire and live a comfortable life. My accountant suggested I should diversify and recommended me to Madoff, telling me of his great returns on investments. I met with Stanley Berman who I thought was a representative of Madoff, (he actually worked for Cohmad) who after asking me a lot of questions said, "Let's go meet Bernie (Madoff)". Bernie asked me more questions and I said, "I am going to invest a million dollars with you and you are asking me questions, shouldn't I be asking the questions?" He said, "You don't have to ask me any questions just check us out with the SEC. They have audited us many times and we have a clean bill of health."

I checked with the SEC and Madoff was as good as gold. I also did other due diligence and every time Madoff was recommended. Eventually, because of his high rate of return I moved all my money to an IRA account with Madoff. I felt secure, as the IRS had also endorsed Madoff. I was able to live on the income the account produced.

My world came to an end on December 11th, 2008. We were having dinner when the phone rang. It was my daughter Bette. She was hysterical and told me Madoff was just arrested. I had no idea of the implications and what was going to happen to me. Madoff kept the IRA funds with a custodian: FISERV, their offices were in Denver. As it was two hours earlier at FISERV, I thought I might still be able to get my monies out from FISERV. I called FISERV immediately but to no avail. I could not believe that the government would allow this crime to go unnoticed. I also thought the victims would be compensated. How wrong I was.

Right after New Years I was contacted by an attorney, Stephen Weiss, who asked me if I would appear before the Finance Committee of the House of Representatives in Washington, DC. I agreed to speak as I felt that the government needed to put a face on the victims.

I felt like I was living in a dream. The realities of my finances were too much to bear. I was completely wiped out. Absolutely devastated financially; left with no money and few assets. Even after appearing before Congress I had no idea how bad my situation was and how much worse it would get. I could not believe the government would let a thing like this happen.

The reality set in when I realized that I could only make a few months of my mortgage payments and after that we faced foreclosure and bankruptcy. Unbelievable. I was 75 years old, my life forever changed and no where to turn. I started to buy lottery tickets.

We put the house up for sale and were lucky enough to find a buyer in a terrible market. We sold the house for just enough to cover the mortgage.

Most of our life and memories ended up in a 40 foot dumpster. Not knowing what our future held, we just kept throwing things away. Our daughter Alice and son-in-law Joe, opened their home, in Woodland Hills, California to us. We left friends, family and community and even one of our beloved dogs, and moved to Woodland Hills. To say it was difficult for my wife Ruth and me would be an understatement. We both were in a terrible state of depression, and both undergoing psychological counseling. I have to say there was more than one time I thought about suicide.

Fortunately for me my best friend lives in Los Angeles. He was at my side every day, with a phone call, a lunch and just being there. Without him I don't know if I would have survived. My sister Linda, who lives in San Francisco came down to see us and thankfully called my daughter Bette. She told Bette after seeing us, if she didn't get us out of California we would wither and die. While my daughter Alice and son-in-law Joe tried their best to make a life for us, we found it very difficult to adapt to all of the sudden changes. Starting over later in life is difficult under the best of circumstances. Bette came out to California and after seeing us told us she would find a way to get us back east.

Now the miracles..... I started to realize even with this devastation what good and great things have come to us. Right after I appeared before Congress a woman who I never met, called and asked if she could help. I told her we were hoping some day to get to get some money and move to Florida. She, a total stranger, told me to go to

Florida and she would put the down payment on the house for us. I couldn't accept but was in tears thinking of how many wonderful and caring people there are in this world.

A group of friends got together and raised $50,000 for us to pay the mortgage in case we didn't sell the house. How remarkable. I keep thinking we must be special to have friends like that.

Two days after Madoff went under, **I opened a letter from my son Larry and daughter-in-law Patty and found a check for $25,000, to help us through this mess.** My sister and brother-in-law send us a check every month to help us get by. My brother-in-law and sister-in-law sent us a large check to help us. My two nephews each sent us money to help. How grateful we are for all of the support and love.

But the ultimate…my daughter Bette and son-in-law Stephen bought us a beautiful house not far from where we lived before. We are back with our friends and community. We have a sense of peace for the first time in a year and a half.

We now live on Social Security and help from our family. Quite a change from the life we once knew and worked so hard for. You know, Ruth and I are the two happiest people in the world. It took this personal tragedy to open our eyes. We are so rich in family and friends that I can hardly believe it. I still can't believe what an impact we had on people's lives to have so many caring and giving friends and family. Going through this cycle of rich and then poor, we are thankful, grateful and happy with our lives every day we live.

There is a light at the end of the tunnel.

Life Is Not A Videotape
Cynthia Friedman

I've always liked videotape. You can rewind, then replay the parts you like, and erase the parts you don't. Unfortunately, life is not a videotape. Life is a long twisting road. You never really see where it's going to or what's coming around the bend. You might think you know, but it's never what you expect. Somewhere along that road will be a sharp U-turn you didn't see coming. I should have known this. Those unexpected twists have caught me too many times before. On a bright sunny day in February, when I was 24 years old the phone rang. My brother told me our father died of a massive coronary. On a cold, snowy New Year's morning, when I was 31, I received a call in the middle of the night from my sister that our brother had just died of a massive coronary. In July 2008, while I was driving back from babysitting my grandchildren, I received a call that my mother had just died. To this day when the phone rings my heart seems to race.

Even though each deadly twist caught me off guard and caused me gut wrenching grief, I still thought I could navigate the long blind road my way. On December 11, 2008, I finally learned that control was not and never had been in my hands at all. I guess I was a slow learner. I was happily chatting away on the phone with my son

75

about possibly attending "opening day" at the new Yankee Stadium with him. I heard a noise and looked up. Richard was standing there. But, it wasn't my normally happy, sweet husband. He had a doom and gloom expression on his face and told me to end the call. My first instinct was a childish one – hide under the covers and tell him not to say anything. "If I don't hear what it is, it won't exist. It can't hurt me." Of course, I knew nothing keeps bad news away no matter how much you wish it. He looked at me with a mournful stare and in a monotone voice said "Madoff's been arrested. It was a Ponzi scheme." I had a momentary relief taking breath. My children, grandchildren and sister were fine. Thank G-d! Immediately after that "relief" I realized there was a "death" – a death of our dreams and all the plans we'd been working hard towards for the last 40 years. I'm somewhat embarrassed about my hysterical reaction and "zombie" state for the following months. I knew better, from my bitter, painful experiences with death; I knew what was really important in life. How it was to live without loved ones, to not be able to touch them one more time, laugh with them one more time, and tell them you love them one more time. As much as you want to, you can't rewind life back to that happy moment you wish you could hold onto forever. Even having lived through these tragedies I still felt my world had come to an end. It was hard to catch my breath and it felt like someone was twisting my insides and then I was swamped by a giant wave of crippling fear.

To me money was never about what it could buy; it was about "safety" – a huge safety net to cushion those big bumps in the road. My parents had lived through the Great Depression. As their offspring I was taught responsible financial living. "Don't spend what you don't have." "Never owe anyone money," and "Save for that eventual catastrophe."

Before Madoff, Richard and I knew we had a hurdle coming up. Richard has a disease called achalasia that makes the esophagus non-functioning, resulting in an inability to eat. Over time the esophagus gets enlarged and misshapen, and may simply

76

disintegrate. Some years ago two top surgeons told us that Richard needed an esophagectomy. The operation and recovery are grueling, and takes about six months to a year to recover. Since he was coping with his food to some degree, we decided to delay the operation for as long as we could. Our fear of the operation was somewhat mitigated by the knowledge we could afford the best surgeon and care for Richard even though the doctor and hospital were not on our health plan. Now what? What would we do? I couldn't lose Richard too! I felt at sea. These terrible thoughts just kept attacking me and the world became a very scary place. I was afraid to go forward for fear something else would go wrong and I had no means of fixing it. But whether you participate in life or not, things continue to happen. Unexpectedly our refrigerator died. Before 12/11/08 it wouldn't have been a big deal. Now it loomed large – another thing to fret about. Then there were those incredibly nasty bloggers and all their hate spewing out at us. "You're just greedy b-----s." "You deserve everything you get." "Welcome to my world." "Boo-hoo, get over it." The worst ones were the anti-Semitic ones. Why are people behaving this way? I didn't do anything wrong. I don't wish them ill. Why do they want to hurt me? The world just kept getting darker and more scary, and I just wanted to retreat.

Ironically, what made everything worse was that Richard and I have always been each other's best friend. We always confided in one another, found warmth and solace within each other. Here we were at one of our lowest points. I couldn't discuss it with my best friend, my love, who always comforted me when I was sad. I knew it would hurt him further if I expressed my sadness and devastation. He would internalize it and blame himself for causing it. He was feeling horrible enough I couldn't burden him with my pain. I had nowhere to go with it, so I kept it in and became sadder and quieter.

Probably our lowest point came when we gathered the family together in my daughter's kitchen. We were surrounded by our true riches – our family – and we had to tell them what happened. All their lives they came to us with their problems and we solved them together. We were the backbone of this wonderful family. Now we sat in our daughter's kitchen supposedly there to celebrate Chanukah with our grandchildren, broken and crying, believing ourselves to be failures because we did not only lose our money, we lost our children's inheritance. We always felt good that we knew we could ease our children's life financially if needed (not that they ever asked or even needed our help) or take them all away for a family holiday. Again, it was a safety net and a lovely legacy we could give our children and grandchildren. All gone in a blink of an eye. As much as we loved being with our family, it was now tainted by little things. Whenever we were together in the past we always paid for lunch or dinner. After all, we were the parents. Now we couldn't and we felt like failures in front of our children. However, it was not our family's feelings. They cried with us and for us, not for themselves. Our son and daughter offered us a place to live if we needed it and all their love, affection and respect. My wonderful sister kept trying to give us money. She would say "Mom would want you to have it," or "I had a dream and Mom said you should take this money." My family is my "true wealth." I can't say I learned that from this disaster. I always knew it, but at the time the loss of our life savings and dreams clouded the knowledge of our core values. Family is the true treasure, but unfortunately currency is still needed in the real world.

We lived our life fiscally responsibly our entire married life. Our main financial goals were to provide the basic needs for our family, have some money for fun, provide top notch educations for our children and save enough for our future so we would never be a burden to our children. We were very proud of ourselves for accomplishing our goals. Both our children had Ivy League educations we paid for and our daughter continued on to medical school which we also paid for. Finally, it was "our time." We were moving on to our next goal, after working hard our entire lives. Richard, as a CPA worked very long hours and the months preceding, during and after tax season he worked virtually around the clock, seven days a week. I was a New York City school teacher (although I love children, I did not love my job; it was stressful and difficult). Richard was winding down his practice and was going to retire in June 2009.

We were going to move into an active retirement community that offered many amenities and social activities. Ironically, one of the reasons we were moving along with Richard's mother and her full time caregiver, was because a few years earlier I watched a segment on "60 Minutes" about this financial expert from Long Island who ran an investment company with some very wealthy and influential people as clients whom he sent monthly statements confirming their investment and their growth. It turned out to be a Ponzi scheme. Many investors lost millions. This story nagged at me because all we ever saw were very elaborate monthly statements and confirmations of buy and sell orders. Nothing "concrete." I voiced my concerns to Richard, but he told me what I already knew. Anyone dealing with a stock broker today only gets statements because stocks are traded in "street" name. If your broker buys for you 100 shares of AT&T, you don't get those stock certificates in your name and in your hand. You only receive confirmation that those stocks were bought for your account. That's how Wall Street works. Plus Madoff got a clean bill of health from the SEC on numerous occasions and had been the Chairman of the NASDAQ. He was widely respected on Wall Street and couldn't be compared to some con man. I knew all that and yet the story nagged at me. So, I decided we should move into a place we would enjoy in our retirement that was more expensive than the place where we were currently living, which meant we would take the difference (about $200,000) from our Madoff account to make up the difference, and that money would be invested in our home. We were doing the same for Richard's mother. She would have the adjoining condo and Richard would be on hand when her Alzheimer's caused violent paranoia episodes. On the morning of December 11, 2008 our lawyer sent the signed contract back to the builder – one of life's little "timing" jokes. Amidst drowning in our sadness over the Madoff news I really panicked when I recalled the happy phone call from Richard earlier in the day that we and his mother were now owners of a brand new condo. What were we going to do? We no longer had the money to pay for the homes. Richard made a frantic phone call to the lawyer to tell him he must contact the builder the first thing in the morning and nullify those contracts. Fortunately, he was able to do that. Tim, our attorney, defied all lawyer stereotypes and jokes. He refused to bill us for his hard work because of our situation. His compassion and understanding meant a lot to us.

One other piece of bizarre timing was our trip to Antarctica we had planned and paid for a year earlier. NON-REFUNDABLE. We were scheduled to leave on December 18, 2008, exactly a week after learning our life savings were stolen. To say that neither of us felt like going anywhere was an understatement. We were sure we would be incapable of enjoying anything. We were barely functioning, walking around like zombies with a 1,000 pound weight of sadness dragging us down. Our choices were either not to go and get nothing back for our already spent money and probably never get an opportunity to go again because it's a pricey trip, or go and try to make the best of it without burdening anyone else with our woes. We chose the latter. It was difficult to even pack. Just over a week before we were eagerly anticipating the trip and buying hand and toe warmers plus other things that would come in handy for an adventure of a lifetime. Now it was difficult to put one foot in front of the other just to walk straight. Pain bombarded us. Times like this use to be the happiest. Now it was almost a chore. There were days on the Drake Passage, the extremely turbulent body of water between South America and Antarctica, that we stayed in our cabin, unable to get up, not because of rough seas, but rough life. When it was time for the landings on Antarctica, we managed to pull ourselves together and go. Was everything colored by what just happened to us? YES. Did we have some good moments and meet lovely people who are friends now? YES, and a year later our memories of the trip are only good ones.

One year later, many hard lessons learned and many extreme emotions lived through. Horror, fear, sadness, anger, loss and rage. I rage when I think about the failures of Congress and the President to demand that SIPC and the Trustee follow the Congressional law, instead of making it up to benefit Wall Street. I rage that we can't completely move on because of the litigation forced upon us to fight the iniquities of the SEC and the Trustee and our government. But rage still comes in large doses when I hear the lies of Trustee Irving Picard and Stephen Harbeck, the head of SIPC. They and their "public relations" team keep repeating the same canards over and over, working on the principle that if you say it often enough people will believe it and unfortunately they seem to resonate with the press and the uninformed. I feel my blood pressure rise and stomach clench as I write their preposterous statements such as "we are doing what is fair and equitable," "SIPC is not insurance," "I'm working on behalf of the Madoff victims," and "we cannot allow Mr. Madoff to decide who is a winner and who is a loser."

None of the victims are "winners." We are all losers. The only winners in the debacle are Mr. Picard and his law firm who have been making over a million dollars a week for over a year now. To imply any of us are winners is disgusting. But they do it repeatedly to justify their illegal definition of "net equity" and their justification for using "clawbacks." Clawbacks are demands for the return of money from victims who Mr. Picard has called "net winners" stemming from his "cash in-cash out" definition of "net equity" which is contrary to the SIPA legislation that created SIPC. They imply anyone who is a "net winner" is stealing from the other victims. Richard and I were asked in a TV interview for Fox Business News if we "have a moral obligation to give money back." We are "net losers" according to Picard's definition, so it does not apply to us. We feel it's immoral to again victimize people who lost their life savings by demanding back money they withdrew in good faith and which they believed was theirs. Elderly people are being tortured by the threat of clawbacks, fearing the little they have left and their homes will be taken from them.

Mr. Madoff isn't deciding who is entitled to restitution. Mr. Picard and Mr. Harbeck are. They have used that absurd statement to deflect attention from their failure to adhere to SIPA legislation.

They are not working for the victims. Their goal is to limit SIPC's financial exposure and hence that of the securities industry. They claim that by using their calculations more victims will be helped. This is simply not true. Court briefs show that SIPC's math will decrease payments to victims while increasing SIPC's coffers.

Their claim that SIPC is not insurance is a "smoke screen." SIPC (Securities Investor Protection Corp.) might not have the word "insurance" in its name as FDIC (Federal Deposit Insurance Corp.) does. But Congress created SIPC to protect investors as FDIC protects bank depositors. If a brokerage company fails, investors are to be paid based upon their last statement up to the maximum allowed by law, just as bank depositors are to be paid according to their last statement up to the maximum allowed by law. If it looks like a duck, walks like a duck, and talks like a duck…it's a duck! SIPC is insurance. The only ones they are being "fair and equitable" to is the securities industry that pays their salaries.

Upon occasion, like writing this now, my rage against injustice overwhelms me, but just for a few regressive moments. Knowing these emotions are destructive, I am now able to push it back from the dark place it came from and move on with my life, trying to be proactive, instead of reactive.

As for the rest of our lives, we're cobbling together a new future. We are moving, but not into the active retirement community we had originally planned. We're moving to New Jersey to be near our two beloved grandchildren, Zachary and Alexa, our bonus treasures in life. Richard is not retiring, but will not work around the clock. His beautiful smile has returned and we our each other's comfort. We can discuss anything, including Madoff. Our life is moving on in a different direction than we planned, but the sunlight has returned. As for me, I am happy. I'm not one of those people who say this horrible thing that's happened to me was "the best thing that ever happened to me." Honestly, if I could I would play that videotape of my life backward to erase December 11, 2008, as if it never happened. Since that option isn't possible I'm moving on with the help of a very important lesson. I had heard it countless times in the past but I never believed it or really understood it until now. "Happiness" is a decision one makes, it's under your control. You may not have control over life's twists and turns but you have the ability to have control of how you deal with those unexpected life altering changes. "Happiness" is not something that happens to you because you won the lottery that day. That kind of happiness is fleeting. True deep down happiness is not defined by wealth or so called good or bad things that happened to you. There are many wealthy and fortunate people who have what appeared to the rest of us as everything, but who are not happy. Conversely, there are many poverty stricken people or handicapped people who, looking from the outside, some would pity, but they have no need for it because they are happy from within. Happiness is not defined by external forces or things. It truly comes from within. After being deeply depressed and sad for so many months I realized I wasn't living. I was just existing. There was no joy. I didn't let it in. I didn't see the beauty around me. I really believed I would never be happy again.

Life really does come down to choices. After time passes and the darkness lessens you realize you do have a choice: stay bogged down in your sad, depressed world or to make a conscious choice to enjoy each moment, each day (maybe not dentist's visits) – choose to live – choose to be happy. I know skeptics won't believe it and perhaps I wouldn't have before. But each day I get up I make a choice to be happy today, to look at the glass as half full instead of half empty. As corny as it sounds, it works for me. I'm happy to be alive, to be relatively healthy, and to have the joy of my husband and family. Life is a gift; it's short – embrace it – live it, just don't exist in it. As Bette Davis said in the movie *"All About Eve,"* "Fasten your seatbelts. It's going to be a bumpy night." But what a ride you can make of it! True happiness does not come from wealth or fame or things. If it did you wouldn't constantly need "fixes" by buying more things, acquiring more wealth, or seeking more fame. Change the dialogue in your head. Choose to be happy. Be happy within yourself. Things and money will never do it. You'll only try to seek more and be constantly searching instead of enjoying what you have. Live, love, appreciate. I do and it works for me.

Gut Reaction
Jackie S.

I grew up in a typical Long Island, NY town. Life was pretty normal. We moved to Merrick, New York, in 1972 from Long Beach, New York, where my parents grew up. My parents meet shortly after high school from mutual friends. When they first met, my dad was a traveling salesman in the furniture industry. His territory was the east coast and he traveled a lot to see his clients. My mom worked for a little while in the garment industry.

I am the first generation working out of that industry. Both my grandparents were in that business. My Mom's dad was in women's apparel and my Dad's Dad was in men's apparel. Everyone in my family worked hard and made it on their own. Nothing was given to them...and for that matter, me.

Dad would work hard to make sure he could give us a nice lifestyle. We were a family of four, we didn't have mansions or servants or private jets. I have a brother too, who was living the American dream: work hard, save your money and build a life to retire.

My mom didn't work outside the home; her job was to raise the family. My Dad had experience selling as well as in the garment industry, since my Grandfather owned a suit store on 7th Ave. My Dad and Uncle, would work in the store helping my Grandfather. As you can see, it's in the blood line to be in the Garment industry. Eventually, they decided to do it on their own – work for themselves and try to make it.

This is where I started to fall in love with business. I knew I wanted to be successful and I knew I wanted to make it on my own.

The business was becoming very successful and they were growing like mad. All I knew, since I was so little, was Dad made shirts for men and boys that everyone wanted to buy! One day, our doorbell rang at home, and it was someone from the neighborhood. They wanted to know if we had any shirts at home, since the stores were sold out. I couldn't believe people were stopping over to beg for a shirt.

A few of my Uncle's children, started to work for the company as well. So it was really becoming a family affair. And it was always fun to visit.

You would think that a kid from a successful family would have everything she wanted...but not in my family!! From a young age, the value of a dollar was drilled into my head over and over and over again. It never stopped! I was in 6th grade, and back then-there was no call – waiting – just busy signals. So, when I asked for my own phone number, since other friends of mine, were getting them or had them. My parents said yes But...under one condition: they would pay the base fee, which was $10.60 but anything over the base fee, I had to pay. Each month, I would sit down with my parents when the bill came in. It was torture. We would review line by line, by line and discuss my responsibility. And each month after the review, we would end up deciding how I was going to pay my portion of the bill. Mostly I had to give my allowance back to them each week, or I would do extra chores to make more money. Then as I got older, I started to babysit.

The notion of the dollar was a big deal in my house. I was not one of those spoiled kids who got everything she wanted. Not even close.

And my mother drilled into my head that I had to learn to become independent and never depend on a man for money. She said "Jackie, make sure you have your own career and make sure you have your own money!" She told me it was important. So I listened.

My goal was to go to a great college, work hard, and make it! I had my heart set on University of Miami and wanted to figure out a way to get in no matter what. I got into the school of my choice. Now all my worries were gone. I could finally get ready for the next stage of my life and the next part of my plan to become independent with a career and financial freedom.

University of Miami was everything I thought it would be. It was fun, exciting, challenging and most of all it allowed me to experience life on my own.

I started out as a business major living on campus. Meanwhile, the values that my parents were teaching me, really helped later in life and especially during the Madoff situation. I was going to be prepared and I didn't even know it at the time.

I met a guy in my sophomore year and we became pretty serious. So I decided not to go to New York that summer and instead stay and work in Florida.

I managed to get some exposure in my boyfriend's business in marketing. He had what I thought was the greatest job. He was in charge of Budweiser for South Florida, working for a beer distributor. We would go to concerts, sporting events, special events, art festivals and restaurants helping to promote Budweiser.

I wanted to work, have fun and make money. I decided to get a job at the Lipton Tennis Tournament helping in the retail tent. It was so fun. I felt alive! I knew I wanted to do this. It was and still is in my blood. I can help market any product and help sell it to the right audience/customer.

My Dad said he would pay for my M.B.A as long as I did it right after undergrad and did it in one year! I agreed! Well I stuck to my deal. I went all summer long and finished in record time. It was non-stop school, studying and hard work and I graduated with a Masters in Marketing.

I was lucky enough to live in my parents' house rent free. They were in Florida in the winter months, so it was like living alone for half the year. I had to pay for my expenses; gas for my car, dry cleaning, going out, etc. They would not help me with that. They said, "you have a roof over your head."

I found a job in sports marketing and knew it was perfect for me, selling women's indoor tennis for the Virginia Slims Women's Tennis Tournament Championships. I got the job. I went on to become one of the best sales people that year. That helped land a job at another tennis tournament.

Shortly after, I was recruited to a men's professional tennis tournament that featured the best players on the men's professional tennis circuit. I loved it from day one.. I was in charge of helping sell sponsorships to corporations, from the title of the tournament to the presenting sponsorship to even some local companies. And most of the players came in to warm up for the US Open which was the following week.

My first year of the tennis tournament, Michael Chang was playing. We became friends and he even met my family and came out on our boat out in Montauk.

I was starting to speak at a few conferences about sports marketing and sponsorships. It was great experience to speak in front of a crowd of hundreds of people, teaching them all about expanding the contracting or maximizing marketing for you and your sponsors. One day, after one of my talks, I was approached by a man who was well known in the promotions industry. "One day you and I are going to work together!" he said. I answered "Ok, give me a call" I put the card on my desk and forgot about it.

In 1995, my phone rang; it was this man who I met at the conference offering me a job working for and helping build a promotion agency. Our sister company would be this brand new internet, at that time called World Wide Web, company – one of the first in the industry. Our parent company would be one of the largest radio syndication companies. It was such a great opportunity. I picked up *Brandweek*, which is a trade magazine for marketers, and at that time there was a small right hand column the new Internet! I knew this World Wide Web was going to be a big thing! I had to get involved and leave sports, even though I loved the sports marketing world, made good friends and worked hard to make a name for myself. It was time to join and help build and shape this new connected world.

We built a company into 25 people and $30 million in revenue. From there I went on to a few other creative and promotion agencies helping build their promotion and internet business.

Then came Dec 11, 2008, a day that I will never forget. I was meeting with one of my clients in Westchester, NY, in the morning. It was a gloomy day; cloudy, rainy and a little chill in the air.

Ironically, that morning, I was talking to one of the junior members of the team about money and how important it is to save. Even if you save $20 a week, I told him that I have been paying myself every Friday since 2003 and that I started with a small amount each week – just to save something. It was important to start building a savings account and a retirement account that was all mine, not something that was from my family or something that was from the Madoff account.

As a child and teenager, I knew that my family business was successful. I knew that my father was conservative in savings. When we would go to the family dinners with my aunt and uncle and cousins, the family talked about this money manager who was conservative, smart, and head of the industry, market maker and a real great guy. I later learned in life that this man's name was Madoff.

My cousin from my mom's side of the family was a trader and knew Madoff. And he always said that Madoff was a miracle worker. He said, "Your Dad is with the best!" I felt that we were safe. I felt that my Dad and family were always going to be ok.

So each week, I would have the money automatically transferred from my bank account to an E-trade account I had set up. I remember my first trade. I bought eight shares of Apple for $13.00. It wasn't a lot but it was what I could afford at the time. I knew Apple was going to be big! I had just purchased my first iPod and could tell this was something that was not a fad or something that was going to go away.

I saw my cell phone ring and it was my Dad but I couldn't pick it up. When I get to the office and I get to my desk, turn on my computer and immediately get an instant message from my Dad. He was asking where my boyfriend was.. I knew immediately something was wrong. I thought something happened to my Mom. I thought, oh my mom either died or was in the hospital.

I finally asked, "What is wrong?" It was 3:02 pm, and I remember looking at the clock. He said "Bernie was arrested!" I was in shock!! "Bernie Madoff??" I said. I said "Are you sure??" He told me again that Bernie was arrested for admitting to a Ponzi scheme. He told me my uncle had called to say he heard from some insiders.

My first reaction was to find out if my Dad had called the FBI or the SEC.

My Dad only wanted to talk to me and my boyfriend about it. He didn't know what to do. He was frozen.

I immediately went into survivor mode. Not because I wanted to, but because that is what my natural reaction was.

I called the FBI office in downtown NY. I said to the man who answered the phone, that my family were clients of Bernie Madoff for 30 years, that we had millions of dollars invested and my Dad was 68 years old, had had a few heart attacks and that I was very concerned that he was going to drop dead.

The FBI was in shock with the amount I told him. He said to me "I don't think we know how big this is!"

I then called the SEC.

I immediately started a website to help others because I was getting the information fast and knew others were out there who needed the information and help. How could I do something? How could I help save the situation? For my family, for others! I knew this was going to change the world forever and that my family was in the middle of this.

I had a pit in my stomach from that moment on. Looking back, I can see I was in shock and motivated by the need to make this better and change it. I wanted to help save the world!

I immediately posted information to the blog I started http://jackiestone1.wordpress.com and had started to tell friends that my family was wiped out by Bernie Madoff, not realizing that everyone didn't know who I was talking about.

I left work, went home to my apartment, I remember sitting on my bed, alone, cold, crying and thinking "How could this happen?" I was sick to my stomach. I didn't want to move. I didn't want to do anything. I wanted to die. I wanted to go back 24 hours and think what could I do different that would make this situation better.

I later went to my boyfriend and he was sweet and helpful, he held me and kept saying how mad he was over the situation. He knew how bad it was, he knew that we were never going to see another dime. He was on the phone with my Dad during the day trying to tell him what was going to happen. He was honest and truthful and even though that hurt, it was what we needed to hear.

From that Moment on, I knew my life was changed-forever.

I emailed myself a copy of all the notes from that day:

> *I called over to the FBI NYC Office and spoke to Joe, the Senior Duty Agent in charge. He asked that I call him back once he got the case agent who was on the case.*

> *I called back at 5:47 pm and Joe told me that BJ Kang is the case agent and can be reached directly at 212 384 2040. I left a message for BJ and am waiting a return phone call.*

> *Joe said he could not tell me much but that Mr. Madoff had been charged and was waiting for indictment. That he was at the court but they have not opened the indictment yet. He also said that there was no information regarding the investments.*

> *I then called Madoff Securities office at 6:24 pm - 212 230-2456- and spoke to a women who said that she had nothing to do with that part of the business and that she would transfer me. She transferred me*

to Erin 212 230 246; (is there a number missing?) and when I spoke to Erin she said we have received a lot of calls, we do not know anything either. That they were doing business today as usual. She suggested that we fax over all the account numbers with a statement - TO LIQUIDATE the accounts. She said that the accounts would be liquated in the am (12/12/08) and then they would be settled on 12/17/08.

At 6 45 pm, I called BJ Kang back and left a message. Still have not heard anything.

Crazily enough, I woke up, went to work the next day. I had a team meeting and told them that my parents were very affected by Madoff and that I did not know what was going to happen.

I also updated my blog and started to reach out to people. I was in survival mode, and I wanted to fix it all and make it better for my family and for those affected.

I also started a Facebook page; Help for Families Affected by Bernie Madoff and the description read:

My family is one of the families who is affected by this horrific man. I have spent the last 3 days working on getting the right information and talking to the right people. I want to give back and help anyone I could. We need to band together and become one. – Jackie

Blog for Victims: Information and Resource http://jackiestone1.wordpress.com/

Jackie, my wife Amy and I have spoken with upper level officials at various organizations and expect to post information about financial and/or emotional

assistance as we can get it. If you know of any
programs, please forward us the information. - Mark

Definitions:
BMIS - Bernard L Madoff Investment Securities,
LLC
FoF - Fund of Funds (e.g. Fairfied Greenwich,
Kingate)
SIPA - Securities Investor Protection Act
SIPC - Securities Investor Protection Corporation
(www.sipc.org)

The case is Securities and Exchange Commission v.
Madoff, 08-cv-10791, U.S. District Court, Southern
District of New York (Manhattan).

DISCLAIMER: None of the information here is to be
taken as legal, accounting or other professional

The only thing I could do was help people get the information and
fast.

I sent an email to my friends on Dec 13, 2008, that my father
reignited his business:

Unfortunately my family was one of the unlucky
ones, who were investors with Bernie Madoff.

From Thursday late afternoon to this am, I have
been on the phone with 3 units of the FBI, 2 lawyers,
Madoff's office trying to liquidate the accountants,
the Wall Street Journal and the UJA Fed of NY
getting help and information for them. I have
actually ended up being an expert on what to do and
who to talk to. And I am starting a help website
today for families.

My fathers strength is remarkable, he is the strongest, saying we will come out of this ok. And started an action plan.

My heart is breaking and I am trying to do everything I can for them.

May I ask, if your company or if you know of any companies that need premiums (merchandise with logo or custom branded items)-t-shirts, golf shirts, pens, hats, notebooks, etc-would you please let my Dad bid on them. He has been in that business for 30 years and usually can get the merchandise fast and at great price.

Thanks again, appreciate your help and thanks for being there for me and my family.

People and friends are the best gifts right now.

Jackie

PS: Feel free to pass this along – the more people that know he is a resource – the better!!

Everything started moving fast, I was trying to get business for my Dad, people were calling me for help, I was calling lawyers trying to get advice and understand what we could do, what were our rights, what would the next days, months and years bring.

I quickly learned that one of my employees was also affected and her father was invested in Madoff. A few days later, another employee came forward that his family was affected.

Some of my parents friends offered money and some even gave them money without asking my parents if they needed it. Some wanted to help pay off the mortgage of their houses, while others took them to dinners and shows, just to get them out of the house.

One of my parents' close friends, gave me two checks to go to Florida with- one for my Mom, one for my Dad- and gave $13,000 to each, the legal amount to gift someone. When I arrived in Florida, I told my parents that I had something for them from their friends and that they had to accept it. When I presented the checks to them, my parents started to hysterically cry! They were crying out of happiness, sadness and complete shock. They couldn't believe that their friends cared this much! They were crying cause they couldn't believe the situation they were in. It was hard- how do you accept money from your friends, when you worked your whole life to be able to live on your own? It is not easy.

My parents gathered a lot of things from around their house in Florida and my Dad decided he was going to take a space at a local flea market to sell items to get some quick money. He took all of his boating equipment, rods and reels, bait box, and other valuable items with him. It was a rainy cold day in Florida and he was sitting outside trying to sell it all. He knew he needed quick money and needed to make sure he did not take the goods home with him.

At this point, we were worried about the houses, and how my parents were going to pay their bills. Where was money going to come from for the next few months? It was a constant worry for me. I wanted to make sure they were safe and that they were going to be okay.

I had just received my bonus at work and immediately put money into a savings account for them. Just in case they needed money; I would have some money saved for them.

I immediately had to change my lifestyle and think about my future, my parents' future and how we were going to pay for the necessities- not the luxuries. How do we pay for food, mortgage and medicines?

My parents have a remarkable attitude and throughout the year, they have kept their spirits high for the most part. A few times during the first few months, I would find my Mom crying or my Dad sad. It was very hard to hear my parents like this. They worked hard, they did what they thought was the right thing.

I remember during Internet boom, people would tell my Dad that they were getting all these amazing IPOs from their broker returns and that my Dad's broker should offer him IPO's. My Dad would say "that is a gamble I am not willing to take! I sleep at night knowing my money is safe. I am happy with 5% return" It wasn't greed, it was safety. That is what Bernie told us. He told us we were safe and that we didn't have to worry. And when we did call to say we were worried, Bernie would say, "You are in cash".

As the word spread about my family, others asked "how can we help?" My standard response was just give my dad the opportunity to bid on logo merchandise. The one lesson I learned throughout the year, was that my parents were very good to people over the years and now they were getting their good karma payback. They always did for people, without expecting anything in return, because they cared and wanted to help people.

During 2009, my dad won some bids and he lost some bids. But he did not make enough to cover everything.

Fast forward to today in 2010; we are plugging along, we are trying to remain positive, we have each other, our health and friends and family who have helped us.

We take one day at a time and try to keep our positive attitude. We do not let people get us down and we have belief that we can rebuild.

A Good Life
Joanne M.

We had a good life. We had just retired after decades of hard work, and we'd spent the past few years traveling and enjoying time with our two great kids and a wonderful son-in-law.

We'd lived in a modest home in New Jersey for 31 years. We raised the kids there, sent them to public schools, paid our taxes, and were charitable. As a breast cancer survivor, I ran an annual fundraiser golf tournament. We also owned a vacation ski home in which we shared with another family.

Over forty years ago my husband had started out as a salesman in a small consumer testing company. He ultimately bought the company, nurtured it, and paid it out – we grew from nothing to a successful business. He was an incredibly generous boss, giving profit sharing each holiday season, and involved in the lives and personal travails of his employees. In 2004 we sold the business for a sum that would allow us to live comfortably and even provide for our future grandchildren's educations. Most of the proceeds went to Madoff.

Why did we invest so much in one place? We were told by a very good broker and trusted friend – "best risk-reward ratio I know". He had many millions in Madoff.

Many friends were also investors. As my husband and I both came from poor families, we'd never had access to anything like this in our lives, and we wanted to share in this wonderful program we kept witnessing. And, most importantly, the SEC repeatedly gave its seal of approval. As we were relatively small-time investors with no connection to Madoff, our entrée was a large, successful feeder fund owned by a major financial institution. They provided marketing materials and our friend showed us Madoff's returns over the past ten years. We knew we'd never make the large returns that friends in riskier hedge funds would make in the boom times, but we believed Madoff was a safer bet to ride out the highs and the lows. After a few years in the fund, we rolled in our IRA.

Things were going so comfortably that we were able to purchase a small two-bedroom condo in South Florida, a long-time goal. We fixed it up ourselves and enjoyed our comfortable retirement for about a year.

On Dec 11th, 2008, at the orthopedist, I was getting cortisone shot for a painful hip. Just as I'm pulling up my jeans, my husband gets a cell phone call. "Bernie's been arrested".

Our hearts sank. My husband started screaming "I have no money, I have no money!" I had to practically carry him out to the car, and drive us home from New York City to New Jersey. He could barely speak, his mind was spinning out of control – how will we pay our bills? Who will care for his 97 year-old mother? How will we care for ourselves when we are older? And the most heart-breaking part of all – everything he worked for all his life was gone – "poof!" We were beside ourselves with disbelief, and with horrifying feelings in our chests and stomach, we walked into our

99

house. I went into the bathroom and threw up.

The year has been a constant struggle to recoup something, anything. As feeder fund investors, we were not protected by SIPC insurance. Even the small forms of relief have proven difficult to get. One year later, we still haven't gotten the $200 a month reduction on my husband's Medicare premium he now qualifies for. One year later, and they still don't believe that we no longer have money. It took us three months of daily phone calls to get a $500 check from our homeowner's insurance company, where we were loyal customers for 31 years. Everything takes forever, and no one seems to care. We are living on two Social Security checks (mine only $800) and small interest from remaining investments.

We are still waiting for a refund on our federal taxes, but will only get to deduct about 50% of our loss, rather than the 100% allowed by the government, because apparently our funds were leveraged and the IRS does not see the leveraged portion as stolen since it went to some other bank and not to Bernie. We also cannot deduct the IRA portion of our loss. We cannot apply for a refund on our state taxes because bankrupt New Jersey has rejected even the posting of a bill to return stolen money to anyone. We lived in the state for 31 years, paid taxes and employed 50 people. And yet the state will not refund taxes we paid on false profits.

The good. In days immediately following the catastrophe, my husband and I clung to each other. It felt like when we were first married, 38 years ago. All the petty daily annoyances typical (I think) of most "mature" marriages, were non-existent. We felt so victimized and violated – the only way to get through this was together. We also realized what a gift our children are. So, some great things have come out of this devastation.

The most amazing thing we've been able to do is ACT!

We sold our home for a decent price considering the times. We "staged the house" quickly, threw out and gave away as much as we could, and had a massive garage sale that earned over $2,000. Unfortunately, we had taken a home equity loan to buy the condo in Florida. (After all, we didn't want to take money out of Bernie!) But we still walked away with decent amount, having purchased the home in 1978 for $76,000.

We were bought out of our vacation ski house by our partner, giving us about half the money we needed to purchase our own home there.

We found, by luck, a wonderful full-time home in Southern Vermont ski area where we'd met in 1969. We are finding great solace here now, in our much simpler life – I bake, I knit – can't believe this is me! Our friends here are far more low-key, no more fancy schmancy New York country club. If we hadn't belonged to this club – we'd never have heard the name Bernard Madoff!

We quickly sold (no, gave away) our condo in South Florida. We purchased it three years earlier at the height of the market, sold at the low. This was so sad for my husband, who is 71 and loved it there.

But we continue our struggle to recoup some assets so we can live out our lives with some sense of security, and enjoy our children and grandchildren – our first arrived one week ago.

It still seems surreal on some days. But we persevere, largely thanks to the Madoff victims groups we've joined. It gives one great solace to know you're not alone and to participate in a group of people who are doing everything we can to seek some compensation for our devastating losses.

This is not the life we worked or hoped for, but it is still a good life.

Starting with the American Dream, Ending With The Nightmare Of Retirement
Michael De Vita

Growing up in Philadelphia my family first lived in a three bedroom row home of about 900 square feet. My sister and I went to a local Catholic grade school, my father worked on the assembly line at a local electronics company, and my mom was a stay-at-home mother until we were old enough for school. Once we were in school my mom worked in customer service at Sears for more than two decades.

Summers we spent taking weekend trips to my grandparents' home at the New Jersey shore. Fishing, half ball, biking and roller skating with neighborhood kids constituted entertainment.

At a very early age, I was instilled with the value of earning your own money and learned the security of living within your means while saving for a comfortable retirement. Starting at about the age of eight I earned money by delivering local sales circulars along with other kids in the neighborhood. When I reached 10 years old my father and I wallpapered homes in the area to earn extra money.

Summer jobs included working at Sears and other local department stores in the shipping department. My first savings account was at the local church credit union. My parents insisted that half of the amount I earned at any job had to be deposited into this savings account. This began a lifetime habit of saving for the future.

After completing school and serving six years in the Navy I worked at a research firm that specialized in sophisticated statistical analysis and forecasting. Many new statistical techniques were developed and 60 hour work weeks were commonplace. I did not earn a lot, but I did learn a lot.

In 1982 I formed my own research company. This new company required the purchase of a very expensive computer and represents the one and only time in my life that I took out a loan for something other than a mortgage or health care. I borrowed $75,000 for the computer to run the new business. The purchase of this computer precluded incurring further debt for an office. Therefore the very large computer was located in the dining room of my home. This was truly a "home office." A few years later, "my staff" was comprised of myself and both of my parents. The company was very successful and within just a few years the computer was totally paid for.

It became clear that this company could generate quite a bit of revenue. If we worked very hard, continued to live our very conservative life style, and saved everything else we would be able to set aside sufficient funds for a comfortable, financially secure future. At the age of 35 I could see that bank account balances were growing very rapidly.

Over the next few years I began to diversify away from bank accounts and CDs and moved into a brokerage account. I found the results of this foray were not particularly successful, predictable or profitable. Returns varied widely from double digit annual gains to double digit losses. I was looking for something with a reasonable

103

and predictable rate of return. I was absolutely willing to accept limited upside gains in order to avoid a large downside risk.

In 1990 a colleague at the university computer center introduced me to a firm named Avellino and Bienes. A&B invested in some type of interest bearing investment with a return of about 10%. About 18 months after I opened an account the SEC investigated A&B. The news media reported that the SEC suspected A&B was running a Ponzi scheme. The SEC investigation indicated that the firm was operating as an unlicensed investment advisory which led to the SEC fining A&B and closing the firm. The investment, plus interest, in A&B was returned to me and other investors. A *Wall Street Journal* article in late 1992 indicated that the real brains behind the A&B investments were from a firm named Bernard Madoff Investment Securities in N.Y. A&B was actually just collecting money from a number of sources, giving it to Madoff and taking a percentage. The article indicated that the total size of the A&B investments were about $400 million. The money invested with A&B was moved to Madoff's brokerage firm. My parents and I each opened an account, funding it initially with the money returned from A&B.

The Madoff investment seemed much more secure than A&B. I now knew that the SEC had blessed Madoff Investment Securities in the *Wall Street Journal* article. I learned that the investment advisor, Bernard Madoff was a former chairman of the NASDAQ and that his brokerage firm did a very large trading volume, as much as 15% of the total daily volume on the NASDAQ exchange.

I also felt a much greater level of comfort with this investment. Unlike A&B that simply listed an interest payment on "something", I now had a brokerage statement each month that showed purchases and sales of Fortune 500 company stock along with S&P 100 option contracts.

At this point I was 42 and my company was doing very well and generating substantial profits. My parents and I developed a plan with two objectives.

For my parents the plan was for the BLMIS investment to grow to a point where it would replace the lost income from pension and social security payments once one of them passed. For me, the goal was for the investment to grow to a point where I could retire earlier than 65 with sufficient income to maintain my existing lifestyle.

For the next decade we watched the investment grow at a predictable rate averaging about 10.5% per year. We continued to live below our means and add to the investment on a regular basis – never making a withdrawal. A statistical forecasting analysis indicated that full retirement for my parents would occur in 2005 and I could retire in February of 2010. The last investment of new capital was made in 2002.

This decade of 1992 to 2002 became one of the best in my life. I spent my time traveling for business and visited some of the most beautiful locations in the world. I learned to play tennis and formed a lasting friendship with a group of men who played tennis most mornings. My mother took her first ever plane flight and my parents eventually traveled to places including Alaska, California, Florida and the Caribbean. The future was bright, and financial independence was all but guaranteed. While the Madoff account never provided the huge positive returns reported in some years by some mutual funds (sometimes reporting annual returns of 30% plus) it also never reported negative returns. I had exactly what I was looking for; I would gladly eschew the very large single year returns in exchange for a reliable and predictable rate of return with limited downside risk.

Something else happened in 2002. Routine medical tests for my father showed some anomalies. Two years later he was in the hospital diagnosed with a relatively rare form of bone marrow cancer.

Beginning in 2004 my family spent significantly more time on medical treatments and the company generated fewer profits. The cancer was incurable. Four years later my father succumbed to the disease, passing in April of 2008. At his funeral, my mother collected the second of her American flags that was placed on the coffin of one who wore the colors of his country. My flag will eventually join those of an uncle who died in Germany and that of my father who served in the Pacific Theatre during World War II.

I spent the next few months talking to accountants, lawyers and other professionals on tax returns and completing my father's estate paperwork.

No one lives forever and my father never benefited to any great extent from the 50 years of saving and planning culminating with the BLMIS account.

December 8th of 2008 my mother and I were in the offices of our local bank arranging to close the BLMIS accounts, close down the business and finally retire and use the resources that we accumulated over the past decades years of planning and saving.

Three days later Bernard Madoff was arrested.

For all who invested with Madoff, our lives have never been, and will never be, the same again. This is a nightmare from which I will never awake. All the planning, all the dreams over a period of decades evaporated in the span of a two minute phone call on December 11th at 8:05 p.m. Madoff had been arrested. Madoff told his sons that the whole business was a fraud.

My initial reaction was one of disbelief. I knew that Madoff had two types of clients; those with direct brokerage accounts and those investing through feeder funds (like A&B in 1990). A deep sense

106

of denial caused me to leap to the conclusion that my account was safe because I had these many years of brokerage statements and stock confirmation slips. I assumed that "it was the other guy" with the feeder fund accounts that had been wiped out.

Over the next 24 hours it became clear that the entire investment advisory business was a fraud. The reality slowly dawned that this retirement nest egg was totally gone and absolutely irreplaceable. As I approach 60 years old, my best earning years are behind me. There is no longer sufficient time, energy or even interest in rebuilding assets that would be sufficient in size to allow for a secure retirement.

I did not tell my mother what happened for three days. I simply could not bring myself to tell her that the income from my father's pension and social security were never going to be replaced and that her income was to be reduced by 75% for the remainder of her life.

Over the next month I immersed myself into learning about the sources by which Madoff victims could recover some small portion of their investment.

An article in our local newspaper, the *Philadelphia Inquirer*, carried a front page article about a Madoff investor currently living in Florida, a native of my home state of Pennsylvania. I eventually searched out that investor and communicated via email and phone over the next few days. Clearly, we were both in the dark about how to proceed. Much more information was needed. Searches on the internet indicated that some Madoff investors were forming a group named "Madoff Survivors" which was meant to serve as a support and information source for Madoff victims. I became one of the early members of this group and began to share information with others. My email eventually reached more than 100 per day. No one really knew anything about how to proceed or who, besides Madoff himself, was responsible for this mess.

We did know that we were part of the biggest financial crime in the history of the nation.

I learned very early on that taxes paid on the fraudulent 1099's for two decades were likely to represent the lion's share of any recovery. It became very clear that the only real "winners" were Madoff's cronies and the IRS. Not only did they receive significant revenue from crime victims, but they also benefited in another nefarious way. Madoff and others who likely knew of this crime paid themselves significant salaries. Those salaries were taxed by the IRS. All of the money for salaries and taxes were paid out of the assets of Madoff crime victims.

The first 90 days were a whirlwind of activity. Realizing that tax refunds would be an important source of recovery, I spent significant time with attorneys and accountants seeking information for what we could hope to recover. The early comments were not promising. It appeared that federal taxes would be covered by a theft loss allowing significant "co-pays" and only going back three years. The investigation of tax refunds for my state indicated that recovery options were very limited. The three year statue of limitation would continue to run while the trustee investigated the fraud. Since the trustee indicated this could take a decade – the state of PA would likely return nothing.

By this point the failures of the SEC were becoming increasingly clear. While I knew that the SEC had investigated BLMIS on a number of occasions I now had more information about the repeated investigations that were both incompetent and negligent. I slowly drew the conclusion that I was a victim of both Madoff and my government. But for the incompetence and negligence of the SEC, Madoff would have been discovered in 1992 and his operation shut down in that year. It was not A&B that was running the Ponzi scheme; it was Madoff. And, the SEC missed the Madoff crime completely in that 1992 investigation of A&B. The SEC report released the first week in September of 2009 cemented the findings that the SEC had indeed dropped the ball and let us, and every American, down to such a degree that they abetted the largest Ponzi scheme in history.

The SEC internal watchdog report painted a picture of an agency that missed many opportunities to discover the fraud. The full 400-plus page report painted a picture of an even more nefarious agency where the terms "negligence" and "incompetence" seem far too tame and are woefully inadequate to describe the failures of this agency. On the battlefield, errors of this type by those who lead invariably result in the deaths of those in their command. The failures of the SEC have already resulted in deaths; most famously the suicide of Rene-Thierry Magon de la Villehuchet, of French aristocracy. I am absolutely certain that the SEC failure will lead to premature deaths for many Madoff investors. The current and continuing stresses, both physical and emotional, will continue for the remainder of the lives of all those who were touched by the Madoff crime and the associated failures of the SEC.

This report implicated yet another government agency whose failed investigation of Madoff would result in large losses for Americans – the Internal Revenue Service. In the early 2000's, Madoff applied to the IRS as a non-bank IRA custodian. Surprisingly, and in violation of their own rules, the IRS approved Madoff to handle IRAs. For decades our government encouraged us to invest in our retirement, both with their words and with the tax code. IRAs are sacrosanct in our society, untouchable by almost all creditors. Yet another government failure led to tens of thousands losing their IRA and pension savings due to the Madoff fraud. For most of these investors, our government has yet to do anything to make them whole.

Throughout my life I chose to follow the rules, stay out of trouble, pay my taxes, avoid the press, avoid politics, and focus on friends, family and career. I am one of those faceless Americans that never seek the spotlight and assiduously avoid any event that could provide that elusive "15 minutes of fame." I am nobody; I am everybody; I am the average American. But I now found myself in a new arena where only an activist approach would gain the attention of politicians. In order to succeed I had to do my best to alert other Americans to the plight of Madoff investors, to make them aware of the role of the SEC, and to make them think about the need to address justice and fairness for Madoff investors. Americans need to understand the risks associated with the securities markets that had rained catastrophic ruins on those who did nothing wrong.

I started this newly discovered activism with phone calls, emails and faxes to a variety of sources. I decided early on that the press was to be a primary strategic asset to reach both politicians and the American population.

The stereotype of the average Madoff investor had to be changed from that of the wealthy, Jewish professional who should have known better. It had to be changed to be more reflective of the many thousands of average Americans who invested in our securities markets with a well respected investment manager and were then betrayed by the government agency meant to protect them from exactly this type of fraud.

I began calling politicians in my local area (both federal and state) to ask about the liability of the SEC and our government to address the damages done to American investors by our own government. I also contacted any news agency that would listen and granted every interview requested by the press, both U.S. and foreign.

During the sentencing hearing for Madoff on June 29th, 2008, my mother and I traveled by train to New York. We were accompanied by a reporter and photographer from the *Philadelphia Inquirer* and met up with a French media team in the subway tunnel in N.Y.

This sentencing hearing was the zenith of interest by the press. It has proven increasingly difficult to gain and maintain the media attention as the press moves on to other issues. I have discovered that the press is an ally that allows us to gain access to those with real power – the political class that writes the laws that controls our fate.

The SEC failed us, and they will fail you. This theme was important, but difficult to convey to the population at large. Only through repeated exposures to the press could we get the message out. All too often these press encounters invariably led to ridicule by those uninformed Americans who saw the news items and blamed the victims because it was easier than trying to understand government involvement in this very complex issue. Most Americans would not even entertain the thought that this could have easily happened to them.

The repeated press encounters, and the thousands of calls, letters and emails to Congress by my mother and I as well as many other members of the Madoff groups has led to some successes.

Congress enacted Revenue Procedure 2009-20 which gives Madoff victims the opportunity to recover federal taxes paid for up to five years. This is a major improvement over the existing three year limit that was the current regulation. But, is it enough? It still allows our government to benefit financially from a crime since many Madoff investors paid taxes for decades.

I have been working closely with members of the state of Pennsylvania legislature to address the Madoff and other financial fraud schemes. We had our own local "mini-Madoff". William Forte (the Pennsylvania Ponzi fraud) victimized almost exclusively local Pennsylvania victims. The state legislator in Forte's district was gracious enough to schedule hearings on the matter in June 2009 and asked if I would be willing to testify in Harrisburg, the state capitol. I was received warmly by the 15 or so legislators in the hearing. On November 17th, 2009, Pennsylvania proposed legislation to return three years of taxes on fraudulent schemes. This may not seem like much, but under current law I would get nothing.

I have found that working aggressively, being diligent and being persistent does eventually pay off. Sometimes frustration does set in which can lead to an audacious act. For me this meant calling the White House switch board one day and asking to speak directly to the President about Madoff. Not surprisingly, I was not connected. I also wrote to Bernard Madoff in prison. Again this yielded no additional information about how he duped the SEC for decades.

In little ways we try to cut expenses. We painted the entire house ourselves and cut coupons weekly. My mom and I actually enjoyed the experience of painting the interior of the home. It happened early in 2009 as we were approaching the first anniversary of my father's passing. It was a welcome distraction from the loss of someone we desperately missed.

In some ways I wish my father were here to share in this experience that draws us even closer together. In other ways, I am glad that he is not here since the trauma of this great loss would likely have made his disease even more deadly.

Every single victory has been earned. Madoff victims need more. And we need the support of every American that can very easily find themselves in exactly the same situation.

A few weeks ago, a federal judge found that the Army Corps of Engineers was liable to the victims of hurricane Katrina for their negligence in constructing the levees in New Orleans.

I hope that sometime in the near future I will see the following press release:

"A federal judge found that the SEC was liable to the victims of the Madoff fraud for their negligence in multiple failed SEC investigations of BLMIS."

I come from a military family. Americans that come from my class wear the colors and fight our wars. For all Americans, mine is the class that sheds your blood and occasionally comes home wearing your flag. I do not come from the class that produces your officers who plan the wars in the Pentagon. I come from the class that provides your trigger pullers. From the doughboy that occupied the trenches in France during WWI to the Marine in Iraq sitting in an armored Humvee manning the 50 calibre machine gun, my class serves when called. When the Madoff fraud came to light it was time to follow the practice of "fight or flight." As all American servicemen do when the need arises, I took up the challenge and made the decision to fight. Now for the first time in my life I need my government to answer my call. I sit here wondering if it will.

I never anticipated that this endeavor would take so much time, effort and energy. I find myself today much older than would be expected simply by the passage of a single year. This has now become a full time job.

My hopes for the future include the following.

I hope that Americans come to truly understand the danger in the markets posed by an ineffective SEC. I believe that the real story will eventually come out and that my fellow citizens will finally come to understand and sympathize with the Madoff victims and actively engage in ensuring that they get the justice and fair treatment by our government that is deserved. I hope that those who were directly involved or who knew of this fraud are brought to justice. It is discouraging that there are only a few people in jail up to this time; Bernard Madoff and Frank DiPascali and two computer programmers. It is beyond belief that they acted alone. And, I fervently hope that most if not all Madoff victims live long enough to receive some reasonable form of restitution from the resolution of this case. And I hope that our government takes up the challenge and fully investigates the complicity of the SEC in this unfortunate saga.

When I look in the mirror I see someone who may actually be considered lucky. Unlike many elderly Madoff victims, I never lived on the Madoff money. While retirement is now nothing more than an illusion, I do have some years left to work. I cherish the newfound friends that I have made in the Madoff group although I wish that I had met these wonderful Americans under different circumstances. And, my family has gotten even closer as we rally around the implications of this government-created disaster.

As I stated earlier, my life is forever changed.

Only <u>one</u> thing remains the same as compared to before December 11, 2008. I still play tennis at 7 a.m. Sunday through Friday.

How Our Lives Have Changed
Stephanie Halio

To say that our lives were changed is a serious understatement. We turned from a retired couple who had saved all of their lives for a good, secure life in our "golden" years, to a couple of people desperate just to survive and to keep their home.

I was saving money from the time I got my first job at 16.

After a number of years working for large companies, my husband opened his own small business. It is no exaggeration to say that he worked 12 hours a day for 10 years, until he felt he could take a one week vacation. Our biggest concern was saving enough money so that we could live without worrying about how we will pay our bills in our retirement. Everything worked out beautifully, and by hard work and hard saving, our nest egg was growing. Our savings made me feel secure as I was the type to have anxiety about every little thing.

We started to invest with Madoff through a family friend's son, who had formed a small group of investors. Our friend assured us that this investment had always been perfectly safe, and in fact, his mother had been invested for many years. We were told that they didn't know exactly with whom the money was invested, but that it was very safe. I guess that I was naive and just took my friend's word and invested with someone, somewhere, whose name I didn't know.

115

I had always thought that I had good common sense and good business sense. This was such a departure from my normal behavior, but I stuck with it. In 1992 I received a phone call from my friend saying that there was a small problem, but not to worry, everything would be fine. We trusted him and had no suspicions at all. Three months later we received a check for all of our money that we invested. We had always reinvested the interest that we had earned so that the amount on the check was correct. The check was signed by Bernie Madoff.

 I had never heard that name before, but my husband had heard of him and he was very impressed that Madoff was managing our investments. He had heard about the great reputation that Madoff had, being the wizard of Wall Street. Along with the check, there was a letter from the SEC saying that since our money was invested with Madoff anyway, we could send the check back to him and that "it was safe to invest with him" and "there was no fraud."

What better endorsement could there be than from the SEC who regulated and enforced the investor broker businesses? Both the businesses and the broker dealers were located in New York City. The proximity of one to the other made me feel secure. I had never read a negative article about Madoff, never heard any news that might grab my attention to the fact that all was not safe and sound.

Whenever conversations came up about investments and we told friends that we were invested with Madoff, they all seemed very impressed. They thought we were "big timers" to be invested with him. We had no idea of how "big or small" we were. We were just hard working people who had worked and saved all of their lives, who did not indulge in instant gratification, but rather practiced saving as much as we could, and planning for our retirement.

When retirement came in 2005, we thought that we were set for life without any more worrying. We lived in a community where there was a man who worked with Madoff. We would always ask him about "what was happening with Madoff." We questioned ourselves and this man as to why Madoff could be profiting in the last few years while others were losing their money. He always explained about Madoff's "split strike strategy." I never quite got that strategy, but that was not my training, and I accepted this man's answers to all and any of my questions. As late as September of 2008, my husband ran into some friends who worked for brokerage companies. When my husband asked about Madoff's business and reputation, they all stated that he was "the top guy" and "the best guy we could be with." We felt relieved when everyone gave him a great endorsement.

December 11th, 2008, is etched into my memory. I could never remember dates, but I will always remember this date. I was entering a movie theatre with a friend. She received a phone call and told me that Bernie Madoff was in jail and all of our money was gone. I went into some kind of shock. It was too horrible to absorb. One minute later my husband called from home after receiving a call from our son in New York City. My husband was hysterical and I was frozen. I just sat down trying to grasp the severity of the situation. It seemed surreal. My brain just could not process this information. I was hoping that it was all a terrible mistake. I was torn between believing and disbelieving.

The first several weeks were filled with tears and suffering. Day and night we were trying to figure out how we could go on with our lives. Not only were our dreams of a comfortable retirement destroyed but our everyday lives were also destroyed. How and where would we live? How will we provide for the basic necessities of life? Food, medicine, transportation, all of these things we took for granted because we had them for our whole lives. There was no relief anywhere to be found. All we did was hit one stone wall, one dead end after another. We were helpless to solve our problems. Everything fell apart.

117

We could no longer make the payments for our two cars. We gave them back but we are still receiving phone calls from the leasing asking for payments. We lost our vacation home as we could no longer make those payments. I started to eliminate supermarket food that I had always bought before Madoff. We never went out for dinner or a movie.

We were fighting day and night just to survive. Our Madoff records only went back for six years. We searched our home, got in touch with our accountant, but he didn't have any more records. We then went through the grueling process of submitting our SIPC claims, which were to be paid "promptly." That never happened, and we were slammed from one financial problem to another.

I thought that suicide was the only answer to stopping the pain. We could see no way out of our misery. Our friends were very supportive and some even gifted us with some money. The money certainly helped but did not solve the problems of our survival. We searched everywhere to find jobs. At that time, I was 65 and my husband 68 years old. No one was hiring anywhere. We were not skilled in the latest computer technology. The only jobs seemed to be linked to computer work. We grabbed at any opportunity that anyone mentioned to us. But most of the ads in the newspapers and online were scams, requiring you to purchase their material with promises of "becoming rich". We were desperate, disillusioned, and depressed.

Whatever we touched failed. We hadn't received any SIPC money and kept calling to find out when we were going to receive. We never got a definitive answer.

We sat in our dark home all winter and in the summer we sat in a dark, hot house, fearing to use our air conditioning which would run up our electric bill. The fear was overwhelming and totally destructive of our lives. We really had no lives.

I entered real estate school after trying for months to get any kind of a job. I don't know how I passed the exams, as I was so anxious about everything that I couldn't remember anything. My brain was totally scrambled. I couldn't have chosen a worse time to become a real estate agent. The market has been dreadful, and in fact, it has cost me several thousand dollars to conduct my practice. I've made a couple of transactions, but I am still operating at a major deficit. I don't know how long I will be able or want to keep incurring my real estate expenses. No one knows if and when the market will turn around.

My husband had gotten a job in the spring through a connection with a friend. It was with a company in his field. He thought he would be put to good use as he had run his own business for over 30 years. Instead he was given a clerk's job and treated like he was a kid. All of the other employees were young people and they were treated very harshly by the owner. There were very strict rules that were enforced: punching in and out for work, from 8:30 to 5:00, lunch for 30 minutes, 2 bathroom breaks daily for 15 minutes each, and no paid holidays, no time off at all.

At the beginning he was very enthusiastic, thinking that he would find a decent paying job that he could continue working at for a number of years. He became very disillusioned when he saw that he was just a glorified clerk and was going nowhere, even though his boss had told him that he "had big plans for him." It was wonderful having some income, but after three months I saw how miserable he was and told him to quit, that he should not be treated like a slave. We were willing to do any kind of work, but we still wanted to have our dignity intact.

Our lives continued to go from bad to worse. No real estate sales, no job for my husband, no money from SIPC. What was going to happen to us? Our son was helping us out, but we had been helping my mother with her expenses and now that security was gone, too. How was I ever going to take care of her at 91 years of age?

We spoke to several attorneys about whether we should declare bankruptcy and we were advised that bankruptcy court would be terrible for us. I couldn't imagine anything being more horrible than the position in which we found ourselves. We had lost everything but our home in Florida. I wanted to save that. That was the only thing we had left and we were willing to sacrifice every other aspect of our lives to keep our home. Our roots and our friends were there.

In April 2009, my husband and I started to operate a transportation business. It was pretty slow during the spring and summer, but better than nothing. We still spent no money on entertainment of any sort. I was back to my old behavior and saving every penny that I could get my hands on. We had lost 95% of our savings and all of our "assets", but we had that leftover 5% and we were able to survive. I felt that we weren't really living and the stress was so overwhelming that I didn't think that I could survive the pain of it all. I had never seen my husband so upset in the 45 years that I had known him. I was always the worry wart and he was the calmer of the two of us. Now he was just as frightened as I was.

Two bright spots were the tax refund that we received in the summer and SIPC money that we received in December 2009. The money was less than we expected, but that was nothing new. Every little bit helped. We have been fairly busy driving, and people have been very kind to us by using our services and for recommending us to their friends and families. We were always well liked and respected in our community wherever we had lived. The goodness of people who were helping us by giving us their business made me feel that there was a little hope for our future.

After Madoff, I lost all faith and trust in any government institution. After all, the government had failed us at every turn. They never protected us from this scam of Madoff. There were so many red flags raised and so many warnings that were made to go away by the SEC and the IRS and other government "oversight" organizations. The government had written laws to protect us, but

120

they never enforced those laws, and, in fact, contributed to our losses by inefficiency and intent.

This is a horrible scandal from which no one of us will recover except the very rich who only lost a small part of their worth. That doesn't cover too many of us. I always said "it's not how much you lost, but how much you have left."

My heart goes out to all of the other Madoff customers who have suffered as we have and even worse. I cannot imagine how they go on and how they keep their sanity. I am still struggling with the way in which I can go on with whatever remains of my life. Every once in a while, not too often, I feel a bit of happiness. Most of that happiness springs from the fact that we will be first time grandparents. The birth of our grandson has kept us going and given us a good reason to live.

I am grateful that we able to work hard and earn some money. We are so excited about the birth of our grandson. I feel so good when people say such kind things about us. Every once in a while I feel a real spark of happiness, though that doesn't happen too often. I need to work on enjoying life more and not being so frightened about the future. I now know that I can only live one day at a time. I must stop myself from thinking about tomorrow and to accept what life has dealt me. I used to wake up many mornings in the beginning of this mess and hopefully think for a second that this was all just a bad dream. In the next second I would remember that this was real and our lives, as we knew them are over. We will never have what we had before, but we still have many things for which we are grateful.

We have loving friends and family, we have our health, for the most part, and we focus on what we now have and not what we used to have. Life is very different now, but it's not over yet. It will never be the same as it was, but we will go on, and not look back to what we have lost, but look forward to a good, but much different life in the future. We are, after all, lucky to have had the "salad days" for a good part of our lives.

We were very charitable people and were very generous with our family and friends. That cannot be anymore but we can make up for the loss of our generosity by being constantly there, as we always were before, for the friends that we love so dearly, and by giving of ourselves as we did in the past, just minus the money. We have realized that many people struggle with their lives in many different ways. We have our memories of the many happy days of our lives. Those memories are ours to enjoy for the rest of our lives.

I truly hope with all of my heart that things will get better for the victims and that there will be some money returned to us to be used to patch up our lives as best we can. I wish all of the Madoff victims much better lives in their futures and the best of health to all. We are, after all, the Madoff survivors.

Picture It
Renee Rosen

I wish I could paint a picture of my life, my highs and lows, and the meaning of my loss instead of writing it. That is because I am a visual artist - it concerns much of what I need to relate. As a child, drawing and painting was my passion. When I received a scholarship to the National Academy of Fine Arts, my fate was sealed. At an early age I found odd jobs to pay for art supplies. When I was older, I looked for work that provided flexible hours. So I walked the streets, knocking on strangers' doors selling a wide variety of items. Carrying a heavy sample case I tried to sell sets of The Book of Knowledge, an encyclopedia; tried to obtain orders for milk deliveries, etc. Inclement weather forced me to look for indoor work-- I sorted used clothing and folded Animal Cracker boxes--all this so I could continue doing what I loved, painting.

After I married, life was easier. My husband believed in and supported my art and I returned to art school for further study. Then, two children were born and much of my time was devoted to their care. We lived simply, in an apartment while putting money aside to purchase a future home. Since I was not an earner, I contributed by taking on responsibilities that would have cost money. So I did all the housework, cleaning and polishing, washing and ironing, hemming and altering plus I gave up personal expenses, like beauty parlors and bought only inexpensive clothing. We drove used cars, camping was the way we vacationed. I set up a tiny section of our bedroom for a studio and snatched little bits of time to paint.

Also, my sense of community responsibility, inherited from my parents, was always with me. School issues became a major concern and soon I became president of a very large, active PTA. I called a conference where we determined the books in elementary schools did not reflect the diversity of our city. As a result the books were rewritten. And we achieved that goal. This was just one of many worthy projects to which I gave time.

When we finally bought our home, it was even more necessary to conserve our funds. So I painted the walls of our house, searched for and remade inexpensive furnishings, sewed window curtains, did my own gardening, but still found time to do a little painting. Then when the kids went off to school, I could spend a good deal of time on my work. I took a job teaching art in a community center and gave private lessons in my studio. All of my earnings went into our savings account because by now we were seriously saving for our future. My husband had no pension and since my social security would be nil, we knew we had to plan for his retirement. I had many art exhibitions but, like most artists sold only a small number of works, which just about covered my studio rent and art supplies. My husband continued to work long after most people would have retired. Our expenses were much lower when our children were grown and on their own, so we could live on his earnings of a short three day work week.

In 1992, the Security and Exchange Commission gave the green light on Bernard Madoff, and after that a cousin who worked in finance recommended that we put our savings into that firm. Since we were very concerned with the safety issue, we asked to meet with Mr. Madoff and he obliged. After hearing that we had no other financial resources for our old age, he assured us that our money was safe with him. Feeling that he was sincere, that our cousin's recommendations came from knowledge, and that our government was there to protect us, we put all of our savings in the Madoff firm.

Up until my husband died in 1997, we left our investment profits to be added to our growing account. After his death I needed more income and withdrew a small sum yearly.

Then the bomb dropped on December 11th, 2008. All of my money is now gone. Where can I turn, given my background, my age, and a depressed economy? After a lifetime of scraping together whatever we could to provide for our future, I am left with nothing. After being a contributing and worthy citizen I find that our government has let me down.

They lied when they said that the Madoff Securities was a safe investment, for the Security and Exchange Commission never fully investigated the company. In spite of all the red flags they didn't bother, and they still refuse to accept the responsibility for permitting thousands to be defrauded. SIPC is not returning the funds listed on the last statement, as the law requires. The government is not standing by its promise to prevent fraud, thereby leaving everyone in this country unprotected.

An Afterthought

We now know that Madoff conducted a scam and his illegal acts landed him in jail for one hundred and fifty years. What about the other criminals who daily perform legal acts that put this country in financial jeopardy. Without restrictions, rules and regulations the huge insurance industry, banks and Wall Street created a system that made billions off the backs of poor people. Many have lost their homes, lost their jobs, lost their savings and some even their lives. If Wall Street hadn't failed, I, as well as many others, wouldn't have asked to have our money returned. Perhaps Madoff Securities would still be going strong. Certainly the Security and Exchange Commission wasn't about to expose him. So we must also put the blame on our financial system and on our government that permitted them to function in such an irresponsible way.

I have been asked, "Where do I go from here"? It's a good question. I have already lost my studio and with it went a good part of the art community that was so important in my life. I now face the probability of losing my home and with it goes my neighborhood community. I cannot afford to go to theater, concerts, etc. so friends, who usually accompany me to these cultural excursions, are now missing from my life. This too means loss of community.

What can I say on the positive side? The only thing that "came up roses" after the Madoff scam broke the news, was the publishing of my book. It is a retrospective of my work entitled "Connections". It was very well received and so provides incentive to go on with my art. My wonderful children give me joy and the spirit to search for solutions - to find light at the end of this dark tunnel.

Surviving the Loss of a Love
Maureen Ebel

A strange introduction I know, but that's just what happened to me. I am trying to survive the loss of a life I loved.

That life is all gone, never to return, because of a sociopath named Bernard Madoff. I am a 62 year old widow and I won't live long enough to ever get it back. He not only stole all my money, he stole my life.

I worked hard for everything I ever got. Being one of six children, in a middle class Irish-Catholic family, I learned about the value of work, and how to earn a dollar. I realized I would have to earn my own riches. There would be no great inheritance or trust fund for me. I never gave this a lot of thought and never felt I was entitled to anything other than what I could earn. I learned how to work hard and enjoy it.

I began working at age 14 in the snack shop of a community hospital that was near our home. This was a great first job because I could walk to work and I really liked the atmosphere, I was wide-eyed with fascination as I watched all the hustle and bustle in the hallways, and I was in awe of the doctors and nurses and wished I could follow them into the patient's rooms. At age 16, I worked in the kitchen of another local hospital and my favorite part of the day was going up to the medical floors and serving the trays to the patients. Something in my heart would feel so good when I would help the patients get ready to eat and lift off the domes to their meal hoping to see some sort of smile cross their face. I think I knew that summer that I wanted to become a nurse. Also, my father had recovered from a heart attack and held nurses in high regard and told me it would be a wonderful profession for me. And most young girls want to please their fathers.

My parents educated all six of us and I did choose to become a registered nurse. Through my first job in a large Philadelphia city hospital emergency room, and I met and married the love of my life, Marc S. Ebel. He died tragically at the age of 53 when I was 52. I have ached for him and missed him for almost ten years.

We married in the first year of his fellowship at Thomas Jefferson University Hospital. There he trained to be a gastroenterologist. Throughout our 27 year marriage we worked hard, he as an MD and I as an RN. My husband Marc worked so very hard with long hours, getting up in the middle of the night year after year to go save a patient's life. As the years progressed, we saved and invested. Because of Marc's brilliant investing, our hard work and relentless saving we began to accumulate enough money to buy a condominium in Florida in 1982. This was something that Marc had always dreamed about.

Those middle years of my life were so wonderful. As we accumulated more money, I was able to pursue all the hobbies I had dreamed about as a little girl. I really enjoyed playing sports and I learned how to ride a horse, something I had always dreamed about doing.

My married life was something I took for granted in a way. I was very in love with my husband. Through our many years of marriage I came to know his soul and learned what an ethical and moral man he was with a backbone of steel. I felt loved, and I felt safe. It ended all too soon. Those first years after my husband's death in 2000 my life felt like a dark, thick fog, and during that time many sad things were happening to me.

As a new widow, some of the worst of what I witnessed is what people will do for money. I felt deeply wounded by the people in my personal inner circle, not my family, stealing significant amounts of money from me. I was experiencing enormous grief and the betrayal of people who were supposed to be our friends. That sense of betrayal was more difficult to bear than the theft. And as the result of yet another loss, I felt as if I could trust no one but family with my financial future.

A trusted uncle had helped me through all of this financial devastation I experienced from 2000 to 2002. I will never forget his joyful phone call to me in the early winter of 2002 informing me that his financial brokerage house had agreed to take me in as a client – it was his "private person who was hard to get in with." He commented that the brokerage house had turned away his friend whose fortune was $25 million. When I asked him why, he said he didn't know. It is only with hindsight that I see I was the perfect specimen for Bernard Madoff to prey upon. A new widow couldn't possibly be that financially savvy and I had enough money to make it worth his while, yet not enough that he would have to be extra concerned with my financial expertise.

I did not immediately jump into Bernard L. Madoff Investment Securities. I asked my uncle a lot of questions and wanted to know how Mr. Madoff earned his returns. My uncle responded by showing me several newspaper articles about Bernard Madoff- the former president of NASDAQ! He explained that his method was investing in puts and calls, and that my return would be steady at eight to ten percent a year. He told me to expect eight to ten when the market was earning 16 to 18 percent and to expect eight to ten percent when the market was down three or four percent. My investment would include U.S. Treasury bonds as well as the top 100 stocks of the Dow Jones index. He assured me that Madoff was fully approved by the SEC, audited yearly and carried SIPC insurance. He even showed me some of his statements. As the patriarch of my husband's family, I trusted him and I knew his motives were pure and he had my best interest at heart. Sadly, he opened that same door to Madoff for other family members and for his friends.

Slowly, in 2003 and the early part of 2004, I liquidated all my holdings from Vanguard and transferred all of it over into Bernie's able hands. My retirement account was over $1 million and I was so proud of that. Marc and I had saved every penny possible, and he had invested so wisely.

After the first few monthly statements had arrived, I asked an accountant to audit the statements to be sure everything was in order before I transferred the rest of my life's savings. She informed me that everything checked out properly and by 2004 I was fully invested with Madoff. I did, however, have a small amount of bonds that I did not add to the pile of monies transferred.

In the spring of 2003, I had decided to renovate my small but comfortable Florida condo that was completely paid for; the advice given to me by the sage uncle and another financial advisor was to take a "little extra" out in a loan and move it over to Bernie.

"Don't tie your money up in bricks and stones; have it out there working for you. You'll earn more with Bernie than the bank will charge you in interest." So, I did just that and started making monthly mortgage payments. I now only owned part of my Florida home, and had also obtained a mortgage to purchase my Pennsylvania home. When it came time for a new car, my advice was to not take a large sum out of my investments with Bernard Madoff, but to get a loan, and make monthly payments. My rate on the bank loan will be less than the money I can earn with Madoff.

I was so proud of myself as I shopped around for the best loan rate for the new car. I had never taken out a loan on my own before and

I was really paying attention to all the details about getting the best rate. So, when all was said and done, I didn't own my new car, even though I could have easily afforded to buy it outright.

When each of my bonds matured, the advice I received was to either live on that money or "slide it over to Bernard Madoff." Goodbye bonds.

December 11, 2008 was a warm and sultry night in Wellington, Florida

The sliding glass doors to my bedroom were open and I was enjoying the soothing night sounds of crickets and frogs calling out for a mate, alligators with their funny throaty echoes, and the occasional squawk of a Great Blue heron defending his fishing territory right outside my door. My, how I loved all these night sounds from my comfortable little nest in Florida.

As I kicked off my flip flops and swung my bare feet up onto my bed to retire at my usual 11 p.m., I took a look at my toes and thought, better get a pedicure tomorrow, lots of Hanukkah and Christmas parties coming up; I have those wonderful new Stuart Weitzman sandals to wear and don't want my toes to look less than perfect.

I made a mental note that I really needed to be careful of Jay's backhand the next morning. I would remind my tennis partner to be sure to hit down the middle to neutralize her shot.

I lean over and give my little dog Scarlett a good night kiss. I tell her how lucky I am to have her , and that it is only 5 days until I fly to Pennsylvania to pick up her new little sister, Tara, who is now 8 weeks old. My dogs really help fill some of the holes in my life.

The phone rings, I think to myself, who could be calling me at this hour? Someone must be sick or there's been a DEATH in the family!

As soon as I see that it is my uncle on caller ID, I fear the worst. Someone has died. He is 79 years old and never calls me at this hour!

Life as I knew it ....died with that phone call.

I slept and ate very little for the first five days after Bernard Madoff was arrested. My time was consumed with phone calls to family, banks, to Madoff's number, the FBI, and my mortgage companies in the hopes of getting some mercy. This turned out to be a dead end and a nightmare trying to deal with disinterested and non-empathetic people on the other end of the phone who were swamped with hardship cases due to the crashing economy.

I relentlessly searched the Internet and sat glassy eyed in front of the television gathering all the information I could. I was so grateful to my next door neighbor, Gretchen, who knocked on my door and was holding an envelope in her hands that contained about ten little pills. She tenderly said, "Honey, you are really strung out and need some sleep." I took one of those pills and slept for 16 hours .It was a restless and interrupted sleep but I was grateful for the rest. Going to sleep at night was one of the worst times of the day. In the dark of the night there was no relief from my tortured and frightened thoughts.

Soon, another neighbor expressed concern over my lifeless appearance and gaunt look. I felt lifeless and I felt hopeless and I felt totally lost.

My family was enormously supportive and helped me through the first big decision: where I was to live. I chose Pennsylvania where my deepest roots are. At first, I wanted to sell both homes because I carried a mortgage payment on each home. However, thanks to my brother Tom, an attorney and his wife Kate a real estate agent, the plan evolved to try to hold on to one property in the developing economic crisis, and fight like hell to keep it. I agreed with that thinking and hoped I could make it happen.

The next two months passed as a blur, as a time when my mind and body were pumped with enormous amounts of adrenaline. My mantra was "survive, survive, earn money, earn money." But how?

Through an oversight on my part, my Pennsylvania RN license had expired in 2003. And when I had tried to renew it in 2004, the great state of Pennsylvania said no way. I was not upset by this; it was out of pride that I had always maintained a current license even though I wasn't working as a nurse. I worked hard for that license and was proud of my achievement. I knew I had several million dollars at that time and did not want to work as a nurse again. The unexplainable horror of watching my husband die will never leave my soul, and there is no such thing as closure. I decided to witness no more all the sadness, death, and dying that nurses do.

Within two weeks of becoming broke, a wealthy trusted friend of ten years, who was herself a recent widow, was so kind in offering me work in her home. Could I do the morning care routine for her 93 year old bed ridden mother? Her mother, a dear Belgian woman, who spoke no English, had all her mental faculties but was unable to wash or dress herself. I knew I could do this sleep walking after my many years of nursing.

So, I cared for the mother in the first half of the day and humbly cleaned her enormous and beautiful home for the rest of the day. I washed her mother's clothes and linens and did her laundry. I also ironed for my friend and even took ironing home at her suggestion so I could watch TV in my own home as I ironed her beautiful imported tablecloths and napkins. My friend soon began to be embarrassed that I had become her help. I was not embarrassed; I was grateful for the work and the money.

However, there was a time that I was embarrassed and felt the sting of no longer belonging to the group where I had hung my hat for 24 years. My employer was having a holiday party and kind heartedly insisted I attend. As her friend I already had been invited and had received her elegant invitation in the mail. Against my better judgment I attended her party and awkwardly "wore two hats." I was not just a guest, I was also her mother's care giver and cleaning person. I had arrived early, bathed and carefully dressed her mother in elegant party clothes and applied her make up. The good jewelry came out for it was a must for this occasion. I helped her into the wheel chair and smilingly presented her and to the guests as I wheeled her through the rooms. Almost everyone attending knew of my circumstances and was very kind and tactful with their words. As I heard them discussing their future travel plans and everyday activities I had a sinking feeling in the bottom of my heart that I knew these were not my peers any longer. I could not make a tennis date, or a lunch date, or dinner plans with anyone. I had no money for these extravagances and I was worried about money to feed myself and my little dog and I had a car payment and two mortgages, my life was so changed so suddenly. Because of Madoff's greed I was now penniless and felt like an alien among my friends.

The feelings and emotions that were pounding in my brain at that time were all too familiar to me for I had been through great loss before. I almost said, "welcome back old friends." Shock, horror, anxiety, irritability, and sadness and worry : these are the words that describe loss, but words are inadequate to describe what your mind, body, soul, spirit and psyche experience when you are dealt a life-altering blow. I had now had two of these blows that had struck me down.

As bad as Madoff was, losing my husband was a trillion times worse. I had survived the loss of my life's greatest love, and if I could survive that, I knew if I dig down deep, I could survive this, too. But why must I go through this total life-devastation for a

134

second time, I thought. Have I been a bad person? Was it God's way of punishing me for my sins? Why me-again?

There are no answers to these questions.

I dropped out of my country club, and they kindly gave back to me my five thousand dollar initiation fee I had paid in early January. This seemed like five million dollars to me at that time.

Going to the grocery store was a horrible experience because I knew I would have to part with some of the little bit of money I had. I began to closely examine the price of every item I would put into my cart. I spent a long time comparing prices and was always looking for the cheapest. Buy one get one free became my favorite and I was always thinking of inexpensive ways to feed myself. Once there were two large tubs of canned goods marked "2 for $1.00." I began to root through the cans looking for anything I might like. I decided to give up diet coke, my favorite, because it was too expensive. Fresh flowers in the house were just out of the question and I became a regular at Costco. I had always considered myself a " foodie " and had enjoyed grocery shopping , now it was an unpleasant chore and a reality check about my new status in life . I had fallen so far with one phone call.

The gentleman friend I had at that time quickly departed, the money was gone, so he was soon gone. In hind sight, he did me a favor because I was fooled by him and thought he cared for me. However, before he departed he had helped me put my car on Auto Trader to sell. And I did sell it with no trouble.

I began interviewing real estate agents in order to sell my home and everything that was in it. The Florida market was not good, but my agents were determined to help me. It became their personal mission; how kind they were.

Another good friend, Jennifer, offered me work in her upscale ladies clothing store when I had any free hours.

I began to tell all my acquaintances that I could act as their driver and pick up or deliver their friends and family as they flew in and out of Florida that winter. I had several driving jobs, including driving a couple in their 80's half way across the state of Florida in order to meet their brother who drove himself half way from the west coast of Florida for their reunion.

Working the cash register for eight dollars an hour at night in a food booth at the Wellington Horse Show I had always attended as a spectator was truly humbling. But if I could put $32 in my pocket that night, it was better than sitting at home feeling sorry for myself.

Another wonderful neighbor, Hilary, was so intuitive as to know exactly what my needs were at that time. She was very tech savvy and could research anything I needed to know. She gave me the great gift of her time and was always a sympathetic and non-judgmental ear when I was feeling very down, which was most of the time.

I had no social life, and felt very isolated because I could not afford to go out with friends. One lovely couple, Janet and Bill, took me out to dinner once and encouraged me to get a little drunk to drown my sorrows, and I did so willingly. When I got up the next morning, I found an envelope they had left in my kitchen that contained two thousand dollars: incredible generosity and insight in knowing what I needed. Another Florida friend, Sandy, sent me a thousand dollars. I have repaid both of them and will take the lesson learned with me and "pay it forward" when I am able to help another soul in trouble.

My friends from Pennsylvania, Marlene and Joanne, sent me checks with the kind messages of "get your hair done" or "get a manicure." Self care in a crisis can easily fall by the way side. It began to gel in my mind that many people are basically good and want to care for you and help you when you are hurting as badly as I was.

My horse, my horse, I Spy! What will become of him? I cannot pay for his board, his shoes, or his veterinary care. My friend Gail, a professional groom, who had sold him to me, had always told me that he was a therapy horse because she had turned to his gentle and calm presence when she had endured heartbreak.

When Marc died, I Spy was one of my special therapists, and I had turned to my dogs and my horse for relief from all the pain. I can remember riding I Spy in the early years after Marc died and just sobbing and sobbing. The gentle rocking of his gate felt like a womb I could crawl into and be safe and comforted. I Spy was 18 years old the early winter of 2008 and was living at a wonderful little retirement farm not far from my home in Pennsylvania. He was receiving good, loving care. What would happen to him now? I could not afford his monthly bills and horses are an expensive luxury.

More kindness and comfort came my way. His keeper, Babby, would let him live there for free as long as long as it took for me to figure out what was to happen to me and I Spy. She repeatedly told me, "Now Don't you worry about I Spy. " Another angel, Donna, my friend of over 30 years, stepped out of the shadows and told me she would pay his way for me, maybe forever. In exchange, she could hop on him whenever she wished and ride him gently. I trusted very few people with my aged, treasure friend I Spy, but I trusted Babby and Donna.

While I was awaiting the sale of my Florida home, I began to sell my possessions in order to get cash. I sold my SUV. I sold an oil painting. I sold furniture. And, I sold selected pieces of my jewelry on two separate occasions. My new status in life was forcing me to think what can I sell, what next can I part with?

When it came time to part with my SUV, my niece from Syracuse, New York and her husband were driven by his father to my home in PA in a snow storm. They immediately got into my extra old car and continued driving until they reached my home in Wellington, Florida. Trisha and Karl had been on the road for 24 hours non-stop in order to bring me my car. After a one day rest, they paid for their own plane tickets back to Syracuse so Trisha could resume nursing school. They acted as if this was no big deal, family helping family.

My home in Florida sold at a greatly depressed price due to the terrible economy and due to pricing it as low as I could in order to get out from underneath the mortgage. I was desperate. Goodbye Florida condo, where Marc and I had been so happy together for 24 years when we vacationed there in the cold months.

After interviewing moving companies I decided to do all the packing of boxes myself to save those precious dollars. My niece from California, Karen, took time off from her job and flew into Florida at her expense, to help me with that job. After days of non-stop wrapping and packing our hands were cut and sore, but the task was done. These possessions were things I could not bear to part with or things that the new owner didn't buy and I planned to sell them as soon as I got home to PA and settled. Karen also loaned me money to pay off my American Express bill. I am eternally grateful to her for her quiet and capable help at a time when I really need it.

"Let me be your knight in shining armor." These were the words spoken to me when a good friend's husband Bob, insisted on flying my boxes to PA in his small plane in order to save me the shipping costs. He did all the labor himself, even though he could have asked his farm help to aide him in all this work he had volunteered to do. It took many trips to load his SUV, drive to his plane, and box by box load the cargo area and then fly the load up North. He then loaded all the boxes into a horse trailer and delivered and stacked them in my garage.

Friendships like these can not be bought; they are earned over the years. I was beginning to have my faith restored in the premise that MOST people are basically good.

While waiting for a settlement, and exploring the requirements for reactivating my nursing license, I received a call from a friend in Pennsylvania offering me a full time job with benefits. I would be his office manager. I jumped at the opportunity for a steady income. We had honest conversations about my meager computer skills and he said, "You're smart, aren't you? You can learn."

My thought was: whatever it takes, I'll make it work, I'll make it work.

My first week of employment was taking care of his car to relieve his working wife of that burden. I took it to a body shop and waited for an estimate for body work. I then took it to a car wash and scrubbed it down. I threw out all the beer bottles the candy wrappers, empty soda bottles, and junk, and vacuumed it, I would show my new boss that I would do anything he asked of me, within reason, including getting up at 4:30 AM to drive him to the airport for an early flight.

I was "laid off" from that job in December 2009 on my cell phone while in my car. This was another blow, but as a result of that I have applied and been accepted to the RN Re-Activation program and will be making my license valid again. So, I will return to nursing in some capacity after all.

My life is permanently changed, and I worry about supporting myself in my old age. One of the things I have lost is the freedom from worry; that I will be a burden to my family when I am sick and dying. That money was my insurance for my care. I have also lost the ability to leave it behind for them and help with their education. I have lost the ability to leave money to The Leukemia and Lymphoma Society. I have lost the ability to move around freely and visit my family that is spread around all over the country. This is painful indeed.

I have made multiple media appearances to try to be a voice among others for the thousands and thousands of victims who are now being re-victimized by SIPC and the government.

I am proud to be one of the victims who spoke in the court room at Madoff's Sentencing. I felt as if I was speaking for thousands and thousands of us who have been preyed upon and have suffered.

Thirteen months have passed since the discovery of the biggest fraud in history and there have only been four arrests. Why?

This entire tragedy was caused by the SEC who repeatedly audited Madoff and put their stamp of approval on him as an honest, legitimate investment house.

The 400 page SEC Inspector General report by David Kotz has declared the SEC incompetent and negligent in handling Bernard L. Madoff Investment Securities.

What happens in America when the government causes a catastrophe?

Nothing.

I have always been a passionate woman, widowed in my early forties with five children in various stages of their education. I married a good man who, because of our age difference tried to plan for the future of his family. I only wonder what he would think if he knew what was happening now. I am thankful that he will never know. He died suddenly from a heart attack doing something that he loved, biking, another one of those uncertainties of life.

Two years ago I sat on a plane with my 16 year old granddaughter on our way to Africa. This was the journey that I had always dreamed about. We were on our way to Tanzania to volunteer as teachers, in a town called Moshe. I had often talked about this and could not get any of my friends to join me in this adventure. In fact they all thought that I was quite mad to undertake such a trip at this stage of my life or any stage of my life for that matter – with no hotels with comfortable beds and hot showers, or any of the amenities that so many of us take for granted. One day I was mentioning my dream to my son, he looked at me with one of those oh mom, you're all talk expressions on his face. Then much to my surprise my granddaughter Alexandra said, "Nanoor (the name she had given me when she was just learning to talk) I will go with you" I could not believe what I was hearing. My tiny sheltered granddaughter wanted to go to Africa with her grandmother. I cannot begin to tell you how happy I was to be able to spend a summer with one of the most special people in my life and to be able to fulfill a dream at the same time.

The preparation for the trip was almost as exciting as the actual trip itself, we commiserated about the clothes that we would take. (Teachers do not wear trousers in Africa, it is not considered professional.) How we would manage sleeping in bunk beds. Who would take the top, who would take the bottom. Taking cold showers and what about the food? Alexandra had always been a

141

picky eater. We decided that this was all so unimportant, we were going to Africa and this was all that mattered. The night before we left we packed and unpacked our suitcases trying to fit in all the things that we thought we needed. More importantly we wanted to take all the things that we had purchased in the weeks preceding the trip, books, pencils, puzzles, paper for writing and numerous other things that we thought would bring joy to our students.

The next day we left on our adventure, flying for 23 hours, stopping in Dubai and meeting up with a group from Canada of teachers, students, nurses and medical personnel. We all bonded because we all had the same passion. We wanted to go to work in Africa, to try to make a difference. We arrived feeling tired, excited and most of all very happy.

After we settled in we all got our assignments. Mine was to work in a prison school. I couldn't have been happier. I had volunteered in a woman's prison for over ten years teaching AIDS education and prevention. My model had been used in many prisons. It was at the beginning of the epidemic. My passion was directed by the memory of my brother who had been infected through contaminated blood. His untimely death came after a valiant fight to survive. This truly was a great American tragedy; so many innocent people had to die before any action was taken.

The time that we spent in Africa was so special. The people that we worked with surrounded us with love and affection. They had so little compared to what I thought that I had. I hoped that Alexandra would learn how fortunate she was. How lucky that she lived in a country of laws. Tanzania is a corrupt country; you are surrounded by people taking bribes, trying to extort money from you. None of this is hidden. It is very much out in the open.

We fell in love with our students and the people we worked with, they have so little and yet they appreciate all that you give to them. Alexandra and I fell into the habit of going to the super market each day after school we bought cookies, candies, juice, cups for the children to drink their porridge from, we even bought brooms to sweep the concrete floors in the class room. And all the time we struggled with our Swahili. Alexandra was far more diligent and did quite well.

We had the opportunity to visit the court of The Hague in Arusha; we sat in on some of the trials and learned what real corruption was all about. We heard about the atrocities committed by men in Rwanda. So hard to imagine and yet all so true.

All too soon our trip came to an end. We said our goodbyes to the children at the schools. They sang songs, made us cakes, they laughed and cried and asked us to return as soon as possible. The love that they gave us was priceless. I made a promise that I would return the following year and so would Ali and this time we would bring Samantha her sister. We have sent e-mails back and forth; the language barrier has made it difficult for me to explain that I would not be able to keep my promise to return to the school the following year. It is hard for them to understand that the same kind of corruption that they fight in their country also exists in my country. That an important man in the investment world in America was as corrupt and dishonest as so many of the officials in Africa. They could not understand that I had lost everything and that I no longer had money to return to Africa to be with them.

My life came to a screeching halt on December 11, 2008. I was driving home from a volunteer job when my son phoned me in my car. He said, "Mom, Bernie was arrested". I answered, "Bernie who?"

He replied "Bernie Madoff, he has been arrested for securities fraud." A few moments later I pulled my car into my drive way and went into the house, still not fully understanding this phone call. I called my 86 year old sister in law (a former school secretary) and relayed the message to her. She was stunned. How could this be possible? Bernard Madoff was the gold standard of Wall Street. He sat on all the prestigious financial committees. He was honored by philanthropic agencies; he was a heavy donor to political campaigns, he sat on the board of directors of financial agencies, some of which he was the chairman. The list of his accomplishments is far too long to mention. People spoke his name with reverence. He was GOD, and like some gods he has changed and destroyed the lives of thousands of people. Leaving many of them completely destitute.

Even though I will not allow Bernard Madoff to define who I am, I have to admit I now live my life in the shadow of great uncertainty. I have received the dreaded claw back letter from the trustee Mr. Irving Picard. The tables have turned and I am now the thief, and I have stolen what I thought was mine. I can no longer afford to remain in my town house and I am unable to sell it. I am of an age where it is difficult to find employment. All I do now is wait. Yet I hang on to the idealistic view that I still live in a country of laws and I pray that all victims will be treated with the fairness and respect that they deserve, that the people that I have elected to govern this country will do what is right and just. Until then, I approach each day full of hope. I have my family, my friends and I am surrounded by people who I love and who love me. I even have a dentist who has offered me free root canals for as long as he practices. I also have an accountant that does my taxes as a gift and dear friends who have offered me money towards my legal fees. I am truly a lucky woman.

Norma Hill wife of Jack Hill (deceased)

Mother of five children, grandmother of 11

Man Plans, God Laughs, Man Learns Lesson
Richard Friedman

My wife, Cyndee, and I had just sat down in our airplane seats. There was something very comforting about this, like a Pavlovian response, knowing that the beginning of a long flight was a signal that we would soon be sharing another incredible experience in a far-off location. We were always at our most exuberant, being together on these trips, far from the reality of everyday living. But this time that euphoric feeling was missing, as the reality of our situation could not be escaped from for more than a few moments.

The date was December 18, 2008. It was a mere seven days after the news that forever changed our lives and the lives of tens of thousands of people. The irony was we were departing on the most expensive trip of our lives to Antarctica; one we could no longer afford. What person in their right mind would leave on a vacation right after suffering such an all encompassing financial disaster?

We had booked and paid for this trip a year in advance and would have lost the entire cost of the trip had we canceled at this point. Chances were that we would never have this opportunity again. It wasn't until just two days before that we finally chose to go and do the best we could rather than stay home and be totally miserable while forfeiting the price of the trip. Though we were at one of the most isolated and unspoiled places on the planet our minds remained far away; we were trying, but failing, to return to the relative simplicity that our lives were prior to December 11, 2008.

145

It's amazing how precious and fragile life can be; it can unexpectedly turn on a dime. Nobody among our family and friends died on December 11[th,] but the culmination of forty years of working very hard, while living modestly, vanished instantly with a phone call. It was the "death" of a life's dream. Millions of dollars of money we thought we had, money that we never had used to supplement our lifestyle, saved for our retirement, all gone.

The caller was a woman, for whose Madoff invested trust I was the accountant. I tried to be like a caring "uncle" to her as I was "processing" what she was saying in an academic way. As the phone call ended, my accountant "hat" came off and the reality began to set in that not only did she lose most of her life savings, but so did my sister, so did my recently-widowed mother, and so had I. It felt like I was riding a plane where the captain announced that we were going to crash, or that I had been told I had terminal cancer with no chance of survival.

"How could I have allowed this to happen?" I kept asking myself. In the 1990's, when the stock market was yielding annual returns of 30% to 40% and skyrocketing I asked my father (who had put me into Madoff in 1991), "wouldn't it be better if we were invested in the stock market rather than with Madoff" (whose return on investment was around 14%-15%, less than half of what the market was returning)? He lectured me that "bulls and bears both make money but that pigs get slaughtered." His advice was "vindicated" in 2000 with the "dotcom" meltdown along with the rest of the market. Madoff, who always (purportedly) took short term positions that did better in volatile markets continued to give similar returns, though reduced to 10%-12%. After witnessing this, I felt safer being invested with Madoff.

As my mind returned to the "present" it dawned on me that I now had to head home and tell my wife of 37 years that most of our assets and all of our life plans were gone. I dreaded the thought that I held the "power" that would destroy the "status quo" of her life –

changing forever. I could give her more hours of happiness or take it away the moment I arrived home. There was really no choice.

I walked into our bedroom and found her on the phone speaking with our son. She asked if I wanted opening day tickets to see the Yankees play in their first season in their new ballpark. I told her I was "not interested." Sensing something was very wrong she told our son, "Dad's in a bad mood, talk with you later." I turned off the TV, knowing that this was "the moment," the "point of no return." For the entire 40 years we knew each other I had always protected her. Now I was about to do the opposite. I was about to "take away" most of her financial assets, her peace of mind, her security, and her future.

Though nothing like this ever happened between the two of us, her initial reaction was, as expected, an emotional outpouring that would not stop. I felt like the most evil person in the world for having done this to her. The "reality" that had been our life for so many years was gone in an instant, and I could find no words to comfort her. I felt I was living someone else's life and wanted my own life back. We wanted back "our reality," finding it impossible to believe that it was really gone.

After working for nearly 40 years (and my wife Cyndee working as a teacher for over 20 years), we were going to retire and spend the rest of our lives being closer to our children and grandchildren and enjoying the leisure time I never could make for myself. To that end, I had reduced my accounting practice and was just six months from "closing the door."

Over the next few days, as Cyndee looked to me for answers that I could not give, I became frustrated and hated myself that I had no answers. The next few months we lived in "Madoff hell." The feeling of impending doom, constantly hanging over us, deprived us of sleeping, of smiling, of enjoying ourselves, and left us with the destructive effects of stress. Yes, we were thankful to have each other and our health, but at these times you think more often of what you lost instead of what you still have.

As hard as Cyndee and I tried to tell ourselves that we still had each other, our health, the support and love of a great family, it simply wasn't enough to get "Madoff" out of our heads. We were consumed by it. The reports we read while away on "vacation" and after we returned gave us no reason to be optimistic, except for one. We had known that SIPC (Securities Investor Protection Corporation) was to the securities industry what the FDIC was to the banking industry as far as protecting the public. The only thing that kept our sanity was a little glimmer of hope that we would get some money back thru SIPC.

That "glimmer" appeared to vanish as Irving Picard, the Trustee selected for this case, and his attorney, David Sheehan, left Madoff victims in shock at the February 20, 2009, Trustee's meeting as they announced the never before used methodology of defining one's net equity as "cash in/cash out," not the closing account balance. Family members, who took out more money than they put in, would get no money back and be subject to having the money they withdrew (but no longer had) "clawed back" by the Trustee.

We needed a "public voice" that could be heard by a national audience to explain that what happened to us could happen to anyone, that SIPC's so-called protection was a scam. The "Dr. Phil Show" happened to be doing a program on "financial scams," so who better than a couple scammed by Bernard Madoff could be a better guest on his show. The topic was "How not to get scammed." While Dr. Phil was most understanding and a gracious host, our points about SIPC were not on their agenda. But, for me personally, it was a turning point. Up until that time my mannerisms could be compared to being like a "deer frozen in front of the headlights," still reeling after two months from this calamity, and still blaming myself for allowing this to happen. Dr. Phil told me "the only thing worse than this guy getting your money, would

148

be this guy getting your life." It took weeks for those words to really sink in, as I kept repeating them over and over again.

I began to question what happened to others who were survivors of disasters ("man-made" or natural life changing events). Such events as Hurricane Katrina, the 2004 Indian Ocean tsunami, Enron, 9/11, the Bhopal, India (Union Carbide) chemical disaster, to name a few. How did all these people deal with a world or a government that could be both cruel and uncaring? Did they just give up? Though you don't hear about it too often, many of these people are still suffering today, but certainly not for lack of trying to help themselves.

Indeed, I had lost my "shirt," but I had not lost my life. I had too much life left to be miserable for what remains. If I wanted to get my "shirt" and life back, I had to work for it. When I was with my grandchildren, I wanted to smile on the "inside" too.

It was time to stop thinking of myself as a "victim" and be proactive. The SEC and SIPC were subverting U.S. laws created by Congress to protect all Americans, should something like this happen. However, Congress remained mostly in the dark and seemingly unconcerned. My hat is off to those Madoff investors who were relentless in contacting their representatives and eventually getting them "on board." Credit must be given to the founders of the various Madoff support groups that sprung up and the people who, like ourselves, decided that they were not going to allow a corrupt system stand in the way of recovering what we were legally entitled to.

From our being very private people we went public, trying to avoid hanging our "dirty laundry" out there as the media would often be more interested in asking us how much we lost and what would we say to Bernie Madoff if we could talk to him. They had their job to do, while our "job" was to get the message out that Madoff was now irrelevant to us, and why SIPC, perverting the laws, was relevant to everyone. If SIPC could do this to us, they could do it to anyone.

We, like others, fought back against a government that just wanted us to disappear, but we also wanted to educate an American public that did not have the information to understand that this was an issue far bigger than just people trying to recover from a massive crime. Whether or not you were invested in Madoff, rights you take for granted are being taken away by a rogue governmental agency changing laws on the fly, in order to deprive investors of their legal rights to recovery. While Madoff was a crook, it did not follow that SIPC and the SEC should be permitted to ignore the laws to victimize the victims again. The real tragedy was that the SIPC agency created by Congress to protect investors had instead turned against investors in favor of the securities industry it was beholden to.

The Madoff investors must continue to work towards protecting all investors' rights, not just their own, because as long as investors continue to have their stock certificates in street (broker's) name, what happened to us can easily happen to anyone. SIPC has shown that they will not honor their statutory commitments.

I am no longer the same person I was before December 11, 2008 looking forward to a carefree retirement on money saved over 40 years. I continue to work towards achieving what the law says we are entitled to, while postponing my retirement.

A year ago, it pained me to adjust my life style, having to budget myself, knowing that before this happened I could choose to spend money on something or choose not to. While I knew what the important things in life were, I found it painful to deprive myself of the "unimportant" things. Now I have gotten past that.

A year has now passed and the good memories of that last vacation have endured, while the recollections of the dreaded sleepless nights, night after night, and the shock of all that we lost have softened. We have grown from within and no longer dwell on that which we once had, and the plans we were about to bring to fruition, that just vanished in an instant. In order to move forward, we had to stop looking backwards. We know the road ahead will be filled with a multitude of uncertainties, but it's also time that we start living again. The only guarantee we are given when we are born is that we are going to die. The rest is up to us.

Survivor, Not Victim
Stephanie E.

I can look at a picture, think of a vacation memory, hear someone refer to party, and I immediately "catalogue" it in my mind as "before Madoff" or "after Madoff". I understand that this is very common for people who have suffered a trauma. Once your life has been so drastically altered, you look at it almost as if it is two different lives. I see myself in a photograph and I can see the naïveté in my face. I didn't know what was in store. None of us did.

I once considered myself lucky. My parents had offered to pay for college for each of my and my siblings' children. What a wonderful gift, my sisters and I thought. The gift of education for our children was generous. But even more, was the gift to us, of not having to worry about such an expense. Even still, we all saved our money, "just in case", so there was a backup plan. We all pooled our money, in a sort of partnership, to invest in the future. My dad had two accounts with Madoff. The first was an IRA which secured his future; the second was the investment "account that we had as our partnership". We received pretty good returns, for the most part, although some were better than others. My husband and I had a conversation at the end of August 2008. With the financial market so unstable I had a sort of meltdown. I asked him if maybe we should take our money out of Madoff. But put it where? In the banks that were failing? In our mattress? We had been investing with him since 1992. He was SEC "approved" and we were SIPC insured. We decided it was best to keep it where it was.

152

The end of 2008 was a difficult time. My mom had fallen and broken her leg and after surgery there were complications. She died on October 10th, 2008, the day before my birthday. We were all devastated, of course, but my dad lost his partner of 58 years. I think losing a limb would have been easier. The only comfort, if you could call it that, was knowing that he was safe and secure in his home, and that he could live out the rest of his life comfortably. Dad worked six days a week for as long as I can remember. And when he sold his small business, he put the entire sum into an IRA with Madoff. Who could have predicted what would happen two months and one day later?

I remember the phone call that night. I was sleeping. That was the last night I had a full night's sleep for almost a year afterwards. When the phone rang at 11:30 p.m., I was disoriented. My sister was saying that something happened to Bernie Madoff. She mentioned "Ponzi scheme" but it just wasn't registering. I hung up with her and tried to call my dad but he wasn't answering. My husband and I went to the computer and as he read the news report, my heart sank. As we read the story I realized life as we knew it was over. I felt my stomach turning, and I spent the next several hours in the bathroom. This would be the beginning of many trips to the gastroenterologist, and I would finally end up in the hospital for six days with serious stomach problems.

What about my dad? As bad as it was for us, we were a lot younger and still able to work. Dad was 79. This was his only source of income, and it was gone. His head was still spinning from the death of my mom; it was too much for him to comprehend. He was in a bad financial situation, with a mortgage and medical bills from my mom. Would he need to sell his house? This was too much for him right now. I feared he would take his own life. I was having trouble sleeping, and when I did sleep I had terrible nightmares involving my dad.

Was there any hope? SIPC had made a statement just a few days later, on December 15th 2008. They stated that Madoff victims were insured and would be protected up to $500,000. Whew, that was a relief. Probably we would have to wait, there would be lots of red tape, but eventually we would be paid this insurance money. My family somehow actually managed to have a decent Christmas, although I barely remember it. As soon as the claim forms were made available we completed and submitted them. Then the ugly truth began to emerge. The "net equity" term became a regular in my vocabulary. I felt so disheartened, so abandoned by my government and so incredibly angry. Not only were we the victims of a heinous crime, but now we were being victimized again, by SIPC, Madoff trustee Irving Picard, the financial industry and our government.

Friends and family would tell me they heard on the news that they are recovering Madoff funds for the victims. No one could believe that we wouldn't receive any of that money. The only way I could explain it was this analogy. You had $1,000 that you invested in a bank CD. You received 11% a year. Each year you would get $110 in interest and would continue to keep the $1,000 rolling over in the CD. You would pay your taxes, and use the rest for living expenses. At the end of a ten year period, you are told that the bank was never really a bank. You received, over the course of 10 years, $1,100. You thought you were FDIC insured. However, you received your initial investment back over the course of the years so you are not eligible for any insurance. As a matter of fact, you owe us $100.

My daughter was so bright and I had dreams of her going to college. Her brother would follow in her footsteps. These dreams were shattered. Plan A and Plan B were gone. There was no Plan C!! My sisters were in a bad predicament as well. My nephew was graduating high school and set to go off to college in a few months. And there were several student loans from the older grandchildren that were to be paid by my dad. Now they were all in severe debt.

154

I was in a panic and in a fog. I lived and breathed everything Madoff. In the beginning the media was all over it, and I voraciously consumed every word, whether written or spoken. It seemed his face was everywhere. But the media was constantly spinning it to make it seem like the ultra-rich were the only victims. No one was sympathetic to these people – too bad if they can no longer afford their country club membership.

But the truth was far different. Now looking back I think it was unhealthy for me, but to be honest, it was constantly on my mind anyway. I was lucky to find the Madoff Survivor's Group online. Everyone shared valuable information and we are trying to get some sort of restitution. It feels good to work together, whether it's lobbying to politicians or writing to a newspaper. Going to a survivor's meeting was helpful too. It was a comfort to know there were others out there like me.

Survivor, not victim. I have come a long way in a year. I no longer see myself as a victim. I am a survivor. There is life after Madoff. I no longer care to know what he is doing every time he is in the media. Unless he is telling someone where the money is, I don't care what his jail cell looks like, what his wife is doing. These people have impacted my life enough and they don't deserve any more of my time. I am focusing on my family.

John Lennon said "life is what happens when you are busy making other plans" and it is profound. In the blink of an eye, life changes, but it does go on. I will not give up my dream to send my kids to college. They deserve to have an education. It may not be the best school, but they will go. My husband and I will have to work far more than originally planned. I have fears for the future, but I am hopeful. My dad will have to struggle to make ends meet, after working so hard and doing everything right to save for his retirement. We have gotten dad to a place where he is okay for now. I would like to get to a place where I can look at a picture and see just the picture, just the memory and not equate it to Madoff. I am working on that. I know that we will be okay. So this is my new life. This is my new normal.

LAS

How does it feel to be involved in the largest Ponzi scheme in history? How does it feel to have to reinvent myself several times over the past few years? I am not really sure who I am anymore.

There have been so many changes for me that I barely recognize myself, and my past life seems like a dim fuzzy dream which happened to someone else.

I am a 53-year-old single parent of two teenage girls. For 15 years I was married and a stay-at-home New Jersey mom who built my life around my kids, husband and my friends. My family was financially very comfortable. We worked hard, saved our money, and invested in Bernie Madoff for over 20 years. In the past five years, my husband left me and I went through a draining two year divorce to try to retain my portion of our marital assets. I moved to a smaller home in my town due to my financial change following divorce, and then lost my divorce settlement in Madoff. Then I lost my father who died after fighting off several serious illnesses.

When Madoff was arrested I was completely in a state of shock. All of my savings were in my Madoff account. I had no assets other than my home. I had not worked in 15 years. I had no IRA, pension or retirement fund. I was planning on taking some money out of my savings after the New Year to live on, and was just starting to feel secure after the divorce when the rug was pulled out again from under my feet.

It was many months before I could leave the house to do anything other than errands and drive the kids to their school and activities. I was in a complete state of panic and anxiety. I kept looking at my Madoff securities statements and the SIPC logo. I could not believe that anyone so highly respected on Wall Street, who was instrumental in creating NASDAQ, could be such a fraud. At the time of my divorce I had sought out the opinions of several "financial experts" who all said that I should not be worried with my Madoff account as "I was diversified – I had stocks in many fortune 500 companies as well as U.S. treasury bonds".

After his arrest, I became obsessed with watching the news and reading the newspapers. I was terrified about how I would be able to pay my bills and raise my children. I quickly started researching how to reactivate my professional license and within a week was back in medical courses. I felt like a complete dinosaur. When I had last practiced we did not even use computers! Things had changed so much!

I spent the next six months trying to emotionally heal and started writing via email with other Madoff victims and trying to figure out how to "fix" my life. I rarely left my house as I could not afford to even go to the movies or any restaurants. I could barely buy food. I did not want to go out socially anyway as it was too painful. I started a new part-time job, hired attorneys to help straighten out my Madoff affairs (applying for the SIPC Insurance, amending past tax returns), and sold my "downsized" house. I realized I could not afford to stay in that town anymore.

Last May I moved with my daughters to Florida. It has been a fresh start for my family. My girls are doing well - they are getting good grades, have made friends, and are looking forward to college. I think with financial aid we can afford a state school. The cost of living is significantly cheaper than New Jersey and we do not need any winter clothes (a big savings with children!).

I am now working full time. I am surprised to discover that I enjoy working again. I like the challenges and the diversity of the people I am meeting. I also enjoy the boost in self esteem that working can give. I feel productive and useful, and proud that I am making a positive change in the lives of others. It is also wonderful to have a fresh start in such a beautiful climate. I feel that I have left a lot of

158

my ghosts behind in New Jersey. I do not have daily reminders of the life I left behind.

I still am afraid for my future. I know that I can take care of my current bills but I am afraid of going into my 60's with no retirement savings built up. What will happen when I can no longer work my physically demanding job? It seems that I am not entitled to any SIPC Insurance as my account is being linked with my ex-husbands despite the divorce. It is also lonely to lose the support group that I had built over the years. I relied on my New Jersey friends for counseling in dealing with the children's problems and issues. I carefully chose a small town to raise a family in so my kids would have roots - so many dreams and plans destroyed.

I still do not have many of the answers. I hope that crashing and then building me back up will be a positive example to my kids. I certainly did crash - more than once. My biggest wish is that my kids will be able to weather all of the challenges and dramatic changes in their lives and not come out of it too scarred to mature into emotionally healthy adults. Right now I am still taking it one day at a time.

The Sixty-Five Billion Dollar Question
Ellen Bernfeld

It's been over a year since the Madoff disaster, that Hurricane Katrina for the innocent investor, a day that will live in infamy, and a day that I will never forget!

I was having lunch with friends on December 11th 2008 when I received a life-shattering phone call that changed my world. Not only my financial world and my net worth, but also my view of the way our system works and doesn't work.

Although I'm over the initial shock and unbelievable anger, it's still hard for me to comprehend that such a gigantic fraud took place for so many years right underneath our government's nose, and that so many thousands of innocent investors and charities got hurt; generations of wealth were destroyed by a sociopath and a systemic failure. And what makes it worse is that the system that failed us blames the victims, rather than taking responsibility for its own malfunction and ineptness.

My family was introduced to Bernard L. Madoff Investment Securities the same way a lot of people find a doctor, or a lawyer, or an investment advisor, by word of mouth through a recommendation from a respected friend or business associate or family member. At the time I wasn't interested in the investing world and how "money can make money," so I relied on my father who was a successful businessman and had gone to Columbia Business School.

I was enjoying a flourishing career as a singer-songwriter; reaping the rewards from singing "jingles" for some of the biggest advertising agencies and multi-national corporations in the world, and my father was someone I could trust and rely on, someone who would watch out for me and someone who understood business and investments. He knew the ropes and wanted the best for me, and thank god he wasn't alive to see what happened on December 11th 2008, because I'm sure it would have killed him!

My dad went to the Lipstick Building to meet with someone at Madoff. He never did meet Bernie Madoff though; maybe if he had he wouldn't have invested with him. I have heard that people from our government were calling Mr. Madoff when Lehman Brothers collapsed in 2008 and the stock market was tanking, and they were asking Mr. Madoff, a former head of the NASDAQ, for his wise advice, so my father very possibly wouldn't have picked up on his stinking fraud either!

Yes, my dad did his due diligence and went up to the Lipstick Building to see Madoff's very professional and slick operation, his large legitimate computerized trading floor, that unbeknownst to my dad was a front for his Ponzi scheme! I'm not exactly sure whom he met with, but I know he discussed in detail what type of investment strategy Madoff used. He was impressed by what they told him and decided to invest some money to see how their strategy performed.

161

Then my Dad started receiving the Madoff monthly statements with all of our investments listed in the Dow Jones index, and all the puts and calls, (his hedging strategy), and all of the Treasury Bills that Madoff would buy for us, and a big pile of Madoff's trading confirmation slips. My dad would go over them every month, and so would our accountant. And after that trial period, and with the knowledge that our investments with Madoff were insured by the Securities Investment Protection Corporation (SIPC), my father invested some more money with him because Madoff's investments did well.

But they never did too well, and they usually under-performed the stock market. I think they averaged somewhere between 8% and 11%. We thought the rate of return was due to his investment strategy, which after the fact became known as a "split strike conversion strategy," which was made infamous by Harry Markopolos the courageous and dedicated man who year after year went to the Securities and Exchange Commission (SEC) with well documented information about Madoff''s fraud – information that the SEC consistently ignored. Harry was the whistle blower that they blew off too many times to mention!

Hats off to Harry, but I sure wish someone at the SEC would have listened to him. Why didn't they? They should have busted Madoff years ago before Harry even started to blow his whistle; they should have busted him in the early 1990s when they busted his front men Avellino & Bienes. If the SEC had done their job then, I would never have been invested with Madoff and thousands of others would have been spared too. But the SEC regularly gave Madoff a clean bill of health, which made it appear that he was running a reputable investment business, and this helped to spread his financial virus around the world until it became the largest financial fraud in history.

For too many long years no one listened, and after repeated SEC investigations no one asked the simple $65 billion question, "Can we see a third party confirmation of your trades?" And therefore no

162

one caught Bernie until it was too late and too much damage had been done; Madoff was a total and complete financial disaster, a Hurricane Katrina for the innocent investor. And just like Hurricane Katrina, there's not a lot of help out there for people who've lost so much, and some people have lost everything.

So, about a week after that life-changing phone call, I wrote a song. It was something I needed to do to process the horrific event and terrible tragedy that had occurred. It was a way for me to channel and express my rage and disappointment at Madoff and a system gone awry. And then a few months later I made a music video of the song entitled, "Madoff In America: An Original Rap Disco Drama."

Performing as my satirical alter ego "Norma Human" I posted it on YouTube for the world to see. That was my way of telling the story of what had happened.

I even made an extended dance version of the song, in which I pay a lyrical tribute to Harry Markopolos, complete with a whistle blowing instrumental solo.

In August of 2008 I had started a new endeavor – writing a book. It first started out as a memoir that was inspired by a foster rescue dog, a Treeing Walker Coonhound named Georgia, (who also appeared in the music video). And of course when December rolled around, my experience surrounding the Madoff disaster became part of the book I had been writing, which also aided me in processing what had happened; the betrayal of trust, the loss of security, the systemic collapse, and the injustice.

Yes, we got screwed by Madoff, and I hope I don't sound like I'm complaining because I realize that a lot of innocent investors lost a lot of money due to our shadow banking system and the crash of 2008-2009, but the Madoff investors lost everything, and now we're being screwed again by the Securities Investor Protection Corporation (SIPC), an industry-financed insurance plan which was created in 1971 after Congress passed the Securities Investment Protection Act (SIPA), which was supposed to protect investors! SIPC is a non-profit corporation; (the US President, the Treasury Secretary, and the Federal Reserve appoints their board), and from 1996 through 2008, SIPC charged its members, which consist of all the SEC regulated broker-dealers, a token fee of only $150 a year for SIPC insurance. Therefore they are severely under funded, which Congress repeatedly warned them about, and do not have the money to cover the insured amount of the Madoff loss. And now our legal system will have to sort it all out, and the victims will have to fight it out in court to get what was promised to them in the first place.

My father was not around to see this terrible disaster and to feel it's aftermath but my mother is, and she is a child of the Great Depression, so this is her worst nightmare. I'm living with her most of the time now, and we're dealing with what has happened to us together.

We're grateful for what we still have but we're frustrated and disappointed with a system that has failed us. I'm thankful that I did get some taxes back from the IRS, but for the longtime Madoff investor it's just a drop in the bucket. It's very unfair and we hope that this system can be changed, and made to work for the people; to protect us; to protect the innocent investor from a fraud, to protect our financial and banking systems from the toxic investment schemes that came crashing down on all of us.

The world had a financial melt down but the Madoff investors are still drowning. And now we hope that the courts and our government will bring justice to it's victims, and help to restore confidence and strength in our capital markets.

Some say, "What doesn't kill you makes you stronger." I hope that's true for me and for all the other Madoff survivors, and true for our system and our country. There are so many problems here and around the world, and it's imperative that our government becomes more aware and shines a light on what doesn't work, and then provides effective solutions.   What's very clear here is that our system needs a good overhaul so we can rely on it, and it can start working and functioning at a much more optimum level and bring restitution to its victims.

MADOFF IN AMERICA: A DEDICATION

The Madoff Disaster is a symptom
A symptom of a broken system
I dedicate my song to all the victims
Victims of poverty, violence, and injustice everywhere
May we heal the system, heal the world
One human at a time, starting with ourselves

Norma Human

Joanna W.

On the first anniversary of Madoff's arrest I was plagued by a question: If I could have known on December 11, 2008, where we'd be a year later, would I have been relieved or appalled? Both, was the answer. And yet the question kept haunting me.

I'm a classic control freak. I was always grateful to Bernard L. Madoff for managing our investments so expertly. We'd worked for many decades to ensure a comfortable retirement, and it reassured me to know that fate had dropped us in his illustrious lap, a former chairman of NASDAQ, sanctioned by the SEC. If not for Mr. Madoff (as we thought of him then), I'd have second guessed every move we made.

The whole subject of control looks very different, however, when your life is suddenly upended. It's laughable, really. Not "ha, ha" funny laughable, more of a rueful chuckle.

Control is an illusion. Just ask those of us who felt secure with a man of Madoff's credentials and reputation. Should we have known better? Certainly, the SEC should have. If someone could offer 20/20 foresight, they'd really have a winner.

Even the question of how we stand a year later is a stab at control. Is this good? Good enough? What metric do I use to measure?

Stuff happens, to everyone.

So, how are we doing? Like many of the other "ordinary" people who'd invested with Madoff, we lost just about everything. During that financially ruinous year, we'd transferred our non-Madoff investments into our account with him for safekeeping. He was so well diversified, after all, and had the prescience to move us into Treasuries!

167

Compared to people who didn't have everything with him, we're not doing so well. Compared to those who did, we're like royalty. Through blind luck, we had "positive net equity." If you don't know what that means, I envy you.

Briefly, the bankruptcy trustee defined an investor's loss as the difference between the funds invested and the funds withdrawn. This was contrary to statutes and precedence that used the total in the investor's final statement, which included the earned income. While it might seem logical that investors shouldn't be entitled to earned income on funds that were never invested, you need to consider that the gains had been real enough to pay taxes on – in our case for 21 years.

What's more, it was easier to have a "negative net equity" (withdrawn more than you invested) than you might think. If you'd invested $100,000 and withdrawn the 9% income for the same period, it would have totaled $108, 000. In that case your net equity would be minus $8,000.

Because we'd withdrawn less than we'd invested, we qualified for SIPC (Securities Investors Protection Corp) insurance and could reclaim back taxes against our loss for five years. The insurance is a fraction of our loss and, it's galling to have 16 of our 21 years of paid taxes not count. But imagine not even being entitled to what we were able to claim.

We were also lucky to be direct investors with Madoff. To date, those unfortunate enough to have invested through "feeder" funds have not been considered customers and don't qualify for any relief. Many didn't even know their money was invested with him.

The night of his arrest, the calculator part of my brain was still on its pre-arrest default settings. The amount we recovered would have struck me then as "not enough." With my adjusted calculator, I'm

168

massively grateful and relieved. So many deserving, devastated people have gotten nothing – so far.

I handled our new situation by going back into a business I'd retired from 18 years before. The jury is still out on whether this was a good move. Starting up again in the recession with no money to invest has been challenging, at times, the pits. But I've been busy all year, working hard, planning. Though the business doesn't throw off enough to ease things appreciably, by our new standards, every little bit helps. And the business isn't costing me anything. Having done this before, I see that as a big win, an accomplishment.

The psychic balance sheet is harder to calibrate. I'm proud of my husband and me for cutting our expenses by more than half. We've been kind to each other through the whole process. When we needed a new can opener, Vic announced he'd order one from a catalogue. Instead of pointing out how unnecessary it was to pay shipping, I thanked him. For Vic, the thrill of the hunt and the arrival of a UPS package would be worth the $5. He's prone to pointing out firm heirloom tomatoes or another extravagance he knows I'm denying myself. "Too good to pass up," he'll say.

Our family, friends and wider community have been loving and supportive beyond anything we could have anticipated. We've enjoyed everything from gratis and cut-rate services to continuing dinner invitations from close friends even though we rarely reciprocate. Financial help from family allowed us visit a beloved, elderly aunt and sleep at night when we had no idea where we stood. While it hasn't exactly made the experience worth it, it's been a shiny silver lining.

On the down side, we don't have the money or energy to socialize easily. We aren't going to the theater, movies or restaurants. We don't travel. We have less to talk about in casual social situations. We see fewer people. I'm so exhausted from working; I'm less motivated to make an effort. It's isolating.

Early on, I made a decision to be resilient and positive. We can't control what happens to us, but we can control how we respond. I created a fantasy of who I would be under stress. I'd accept the immutable, roll up my sleeves and move forward. A year later, I'm still not sure if I'm measuring up. In that fantasy, I was much further along at this point. The indicators were more clearly positive. Now I see I can't control the timetable. I'm trying to be sanguine about it. "Try" is such a weasel.

I'm still asking myself how all this happened. I was blessed or cursed to have loved the life I'd been living. At times, I miss it the way I miss my dead parents and friends, with a longing so impossible to assuage it's hard to breathe.

I imagine, if I could flip through the calendar for a peek at December 11, 2010, I'd be relieved and appalled all over again. If I'm lucky, that is.

In The Name Of The SEC, The IRS And The SIPC, Amen
Steven Norton

After my partner Marty's middle brother died suddenly, we attended a memorial service for him on December 11, 2008. Like many modern families, theirs was anything but Orthodox, yet traditions are respected and maintained. Everybody got through it; and his widow, who is an astoundingly energetic person, hosted a luncheon afterwards at their house.

Marty, my partner of 40 years, and I left in the afternoon. We drove back to Fort Lauderdale from Miami without much conversation. There are unresolved issues at any death, and his was no exception. When we got back, I checked phone messages and found one from a broker in New York: "Have you heard the news? Bernie Madoff was arrested today for fraud." I called Marty's sister-in-law in Miami to break the news. Some of the mourners were still there. I heard somebody shriek, "Oh my god, what are we going to do." Two days after her husband died, the widow we had just left found out she was broke and her late husband's brothers lost their retirement funds including our own.

171

We were investors with Madoff who lost our life savings, but ironically we were all "net winners" according to a questionable interpretation of "net equity" that would later come to threaten us. We were Leona Helmsey's "little people" who dutifully paid taxes year after year on Bernie's consistent returns. And we were in shock: Years and years of scraping enough together hoping Bernie would accept our money was wasted. Gone. It wasn't Black Friday. It wasn't 1929. It was a monster who charmed 15,000 "clients" into believing he was the safe, reliable golden calf.

Madoff was first recommended to us in 1992, ironically the year that an investigator waved the first red flag at the SEC alerting the agency that Bernie couldn't be doing what he said he was. I went to the New York Public Library to "research" him. It was, after all, our life savings we were considering giving him. All I could find was a *New York Times* article saying something about nobody knows how he does it, but he does. He was very well respected in the investment community, a market innovator, and he had the blessing of the SEC. With a gulp, a prayer and high hopes we wrote the biggest check of our lives to BLMIS.

For seventeen years, Bernie proved himself. Month after month our statements detailed trades in stocks and funds that were dazzling in their sweep: Wal-Mart, Exxon, Intel, Johnson & Johnson, Merck, Microsoft, Philip Morris, AT&T, United Technologies, Google, and so on. And when the market was down, he put everything into Treasury bills. They didn't make much, just a temporary measure Bernie took putting our money in the safest place you could – our government – while conditions elsewhere were unfavorable. You could do far better in riskier investments, but Bernie was safe.

It didn't sink in until the next day after his arrest that the retirement fund Marty and I used to talk about quietly as if somebody was listening was gone. We didn't want the neighbors to hear us discussing our million dollars. We didn't come from millions of dollars. We didn't live with millions of dollars. We lived with people like ourselves – middle class people who worked damned hard to earn a buck. And it was gone together with our tomorrows.

I remember during the sentencing in the summer of 2009, I wrote to Judge Denny Chin asking that no lenience be shown the bastard. I said, "He took the rest of our lives. Don't give him his back."

He got over a hundred years, but you know what . . . there was no satisfaction in that for me. He was just another thief contributing to the failure of the promise we thought this country was. He was another American screwing his countrymen and a lot of his own brethren along the way.

Harry Markopolos, the whistleblower, in his Congressional testimony said the SEC couldn't find the playing field if you put the whole lot of them in a sports stadium. Several times over the years the agency cleared Bernie of suspicion because they either had good reasons of their own to do so or they didn't have the resources to check him out. Somewhere around 2006, the SEC announced it had exhaustively investigated the last complaint it could give any credence to, and declared him Saint Bernie – clean and pure as the driven snow for all to know – including we investors. Now it's coming to light that the SEC may not have been a bunch of saints either. After being raked over the coals at those congressional hearings, the SEC pleaded *mea culpa* and urgently pledged reform. A year later nothing has happened except a few lame proposals that have faded already.

SIPA, the Security Investors Protection Act established by Congress to maintain confidence in our markets and to protect investors from fraudulent activity, was supposedly the first line of defense for victims. Previously supported by a paltry $150.00 annual fee per Wall Street member firm, which entitled them to proudly display "Member of SIPC" on their logos and monthly statements, SIPC suddenly found out it "didn't have enough money" to pay the claims of Bernie's clients – each of whom, including Marty and I, was supposed to be entitled to a reimbursement of up to $500,000 in securities including $100,000 in cash, if appropriate.

But at 9,000 claims, poor old SIPC realized it would be out of money and probably existence if it honored its promise. SIPC's definitions about responsibilities were quickly rewritten. Investors who, by SIPC's stated position, had a reasonable expectation to believe securities they were told were purchased on their behalf actually existed, were no longer entitled to have those securities restored to them nor the equivalent value of those securities in cash if the securities were no longer available. As a matter of fact, they might have to give money back - money they used to live on, sometimes for years. The law firm denying those claims, in the meantime, is billing SIPC close to a million dollars a week, money that's coming right out of the pot to reimburse investors.

Then there's the IRS. The initials alone are enough to strike fear in the hearts of the most stalwart among us. We've paid our taxes to the IRS as long as we can remember. For Madoff customers, we paid on income that didn't exist since the fateful day we first sent Bernie a check. Magnanimously, the IRS has allowed us to file amended returns for the past five years instead of the usual three - not because it had any particular sympathy for us. They just decided to include us in a provision of the economic stimulus package of our day. The rest of our invested years went ignored.

With a few notable exceptions, particularly Senator Charles Schumer of New York, our senators and congressmen have looked the other way when we've pleaded for help. Investors' letters to the president have been completely ignored. Granted he has two wars to deal with and other issues on his desk, but a simple acknowledgement that we exist might have made us feel recognized if not assisted.

Bitter? You bet. The government strikes out with the SEC, SIPC and the IRS and we lose the game. Maybe from their perspective they see it differently. Maybe they think they won the trifecta. From here it looks like they did.

Personally we're dealing with the potential loss of our home, our dignity and the little bit of security we thought we had for the last part of our lives. We haven't lost our home yet because it's paid for, but if SIPC gets away with claw backs - the term for taking back money we believed was ours - the house will have to go. We'll even learn to live with that. Forty years of making it home, but I know somehow we'll get by that, too. We're expecting the worst, but we're survivors. Most of us are. It's the loss of faith in this country that's the hardest to take, the realization that we're no different from other failed experiments.

I have a copy of an article from *Barrons Magazine* on my desk from my Madoff file, which holds every statement since 1992. Every statement since 1992 is there. The article is dated May 1, 2001. Its trendy title is "Don't Ask, Don't Tell". In the margin there is a note from Marty's brother who died two days before Madoff was arrested: "Dear Marty – Finding Bernie is your birthday present". Marty's birthday is May 3. There haven't been many happy returns of the day.

Dreams Dissolved, My Parents Story
Robin Jungreis Swernoff

The past thirteen months have been the most stressful and upsetting of my life. Early last December 2008 we had just returned from a glorious and wonderful week in Punta Cana celebrating my oldest son's wedding. Our party of guests was 80 loving family members and friends. My son had all of his elderly grandparents present, as did his bride. We blissfully enjoyed a week of fun and beauty, coming together for the exciting first wedding in a new generation. And my wonderful parents were as generous as ever with their wedding gift to their oldest grandson.

My parents are now both in their eighties. They are first generation Americans, the children of European immigrants who were escaping poverty and persecution, seeking their destiny in a new world. My paternal grandparents, Estelle and Morris, were both Hungarian and from large Orthodox Jewish families who found their way to the United States during the early twentieth Century. After their marriage they settled in Borough Park, in Brooklyn, New York. Morris maintained his strict Orthodoxy throughout his life and was in the clothing manufacturing business; Stella ran the

176

household and the candy store, and was a strong, intelligent and pious woman. They struggled to raise four sons in modest fashion during the Great Depression, frequently taking in cousins, brothers, uncles, anyone needing someplace to live. All four sons served their country during World War II, and incredibly all came home unharmed. My father was part of the Fifth Army forces that landed at Anzio, Italy and marched on to liberate Rome. During battle he earned a Bronze Star for extraordinary bravery under enemy fire. My father and uncles all went to college, married, and settled in the Northeast with their families.

My mother's parents, Betty and Lou, were also European; my grandfather was a teen-age water carrier for the Russian army during World War I, escaping to the United States after being wounded, and my grandmother left Germany with her family as a young girl. Lou, an orphan, was separated from his three siblings when he left his home and did not see them again for nearly fifty years. I can still remember being a small girl meeting the ship carrying his sister from Israel to New York for his son's wedding! And Betty was always the family darling, a warm and beautiful woman who loved to laugh, loved to read, was generous with her emotions, and taught me to knit. Betty and Lou, too, settled in Borough Park and raised their family of three near my grandmother's parents, brother and sister. And they were also able to see their children attend college, marry, and raise families in the Northeast. My sister, cousins, and I number seventeen. Like many second generation Americans, we have scattered now throughout the country but remain close in spirit.

My father and his brothers went to college on the G.I. bill, while my mother, an aspiring concert pianist, started at Julliard School of Music in New York City. She eventually decided on a more conventional education and attended Brooklyn College where she met my father. They married, settled in Brooklyn, and I was born in late 1951. A few years later, like so many other young post-war couples, my parents decided to leave the city and move to Long Island where my father began a construction company building small single-family homes for the newly burgeoning post-war population in New Jersey and on Long Island, and made a modest living. He built our home in Huntington, New York, where my younger sister and I were raised. We had a great large yard, many neighborhood playmates, and excellent schools. My mother was a stay-at-home mom who volunteered at the local hospital, in the schools, and community groups. She had a flair for drama and loved acting in local theater, had a wonderful and supportive circle of friends, and considered her job - raising two daughters - to be more important than anything she could do. We had warm, loving parents and a story-book 1950s childhood.

By the time my sister and I were in our teens, with his twin brother as his partner, my father shifted his focus from home building and bought land to build light industrial properties on eastern Long Island. As Long Island boomed throughout the late 1960s and 1970s, he was able to build small industrial parks and realize his American Dream – he felt successful with a very comfortable income that enabled my sister and me to attend the best colleges, my parents to travel, and even buy a condo in Florida.

And the retirement plan? Investing with Bernie Madoff.

In those days, the mid-1980s, to invest with BLMIS, you had to know someone who could "get you in." It was thought to be a very small private investment fund with good solid returns, run by a well-respected financial wizard. On the advice of a close personal friend and investor who lauded Bernie Madoff, my father and uncle started with modest initial deposits which they added to in the early 1990s after selling their properties and dissolving their business.

By now, my sister and I had married, were working hard, and were raising our own families. Based on the steady returns and solid growth of BLMIS, my parents eventually decided to invest all of their money in their BLMIS accounts – this was their income to live on during their retirement. The returns appeared good and solid and were now the <u>only</u> source of income for my parents. They were able to lead active lives, golfing and traveling, taking life-long learning courses, and were always generous with charities as well their family. They helped us buy homes, invited us on their travels, helped us start businesses, and sent their five grandchildren to college. They've even helped their grandchildren buy homes and start businesses. They believed in giving "with a warm hand," and practiced what they preached. Over the years their investments with BLMIS grew – nothing dramatic, but nice and steady – and we thought Bernie was a genius. Trusts were set up and we had a wonderful sense of security for ourselves and our families.

Back to December 2008: We'd all returned home and were reveling in the happiness from our son's wedding. That particular week, my sister was attending another wedding in Mexico and I had been strongly admonished not to call her unless there was an emergency (always possible with elderly parents). But it was she who called me. I was actually having my hair cut when I heard her say, "Bernie Madoff has been arrested." Although I didn't really take it all in immediately, I think in the back of my mind I understood what this meant. I could barely sit still as the air was sucked from the room, and I was anxious to get home and see the news. The phone calls were furiously flying back and forth. After years of believing that my parents were one of a few dozen investors, it was numbing to learn the true numbers involved and to understand the scope of devastation to peoples' lives, to foundations, and charities, to fully comprehend what was happening. The realization that everything had vaporized, all of my parents' investments and their only source of income, came quickly and hit hard. We were so worried for our parents – for their reaction to every vacillation in this chain of events, for their lives and well-being. What would we do and how would they live? Who should we call?

"Well, not to worry," my brother-in-law (a long time professional in the financial industry) said – "there is SIPC! At least that's something of a safety net for investors, like an insurance policy. BLMIS was a SIPC member! It says so right on the statements –

there's the official seal! There will be some relief and it will get taken care of quickly – they cannot delay those payments and we know so very many people are in such desperate circumstances. And look right here on these November, 2008 statements – it says exactly what is in each account." Oh, what relief!

So now we've spent months talking to attorneys and accountants, learning from blogs and survivor groups, writing letters to judges and our elected representatives in Congress, watching legislative hearings, and learning about the sham of SIPC and the utter failure and negligence of the SEC. My sister and I spent hours, days, and weeks combing through whatever records still existed, trying to organize everything for the attorneys and accountants. We learned about statutes and regulations, we hired attorneys and filed claims, and we have been glued to the internet for thirteen months searching for any slight thread of hope. For many months we've all been on a psychological roller-coaster with a glimmer of hope, some small ray, followed by yet more grim news. As expected like so many other long-term investors, our parents' claims based on their net equity have been denied, a capricious re-interpretation of laws and statutes by the very people and agencies charged to protect these same claims.

Under the best circumstances my parents are aging and becoming ever more fragile. They suffer from a variety of health problems – some more severe than others – including diabetes, heart disease, kidney disease, hip fractures, and assorted additional maladies of the elderly. In the last year, my father's diabetes has become far more difficult to control and he has suffered a heart attack and a stroke. My mother, for the first time in her life, is being treated for depression. My parents are scared and nervous every single day. Their lives have become circumscribed by their severely reduced economic circumstances, which is compromising their already fragile health. My sister and I have also been affected by stress-related ailments and have become pre-occupied with our parents' safety and well-being every minute of every day. We have made several emergency trips to Florida to be with our parents during crises. We are working hard at preserving what little resources they have left while still allowing them to enjoy their lives in their own home. For many years my parents thought they would have no financial worries with a legacy left for their children and grandchildren. They have now spent a substantial sum trying to recover their <u>own</u> money, and while they have realized some income tax refunds, they are faced with very scary questions about the future and a very different fate than they had ever imagined. We pray that their health does not decline further and require care they can no longer afford.

My parents worked hard and were proud, productive citizens for many years. My father served his country with pride and without question. He and his brother began a construction business, took the risk associated with building and leasing properties, and sold their business to use the proceeds for their retirement and their children's future. They did not have a company or government pension to see them through retirement years and had to rely on their own resources; so they invested wisely, they thought, with an investment company that had a proven track record and received the stamp of approval as a legitimate investment fund from every regulating agency charged with that task. The last thirteen months have taught us how unknowingly vulnerable American investors truly are. Red flags and whistle blowers, calling attention to irregularities with BLMIS, were ignored by powerful, ineffective and corrupt regulating agencies. We now know my parents will never recover the full amounts in their BLMIS accounts, but did expect SIPC would cover the statutory insured amount against this massive fraud, just as FDIC insurance covers a savings account. We await the outcome of lawsuits and appeals, which will take many more years, and can only hope my parents live long enough and stay healthy enough to pass through this purgatory and recover the SIPC insurance rightly due.

What A Day, What A Year
Lyn S

It was a Thursday in December 2008.

The sun was streaming through my bedroom windows. I planned no work, just a personal day. I started the day off with a walk around the neighborhood. After breakfast, golf with my usual foursome. My day progressed as planned. I played really well and was looking forward to entering my score for handicapping. While driving I was thinking I still had time to get a swim in before dinner.

The trip home was going to take about 45 minutes. This was my third year in a new area of Florida and I was thinking I had made the right choice moving here. I was living in a recently built gated community and was making friends quickly. Living in a house suited my lifestyle more so than living in a high-rise. Finally, I had a home large enough for family and friends to stay and visit. Many evenings I could sit in the screened-in patio and read a book, and occasionally peer up at the calm lake. I would just walk out the front door and look into the clear sky and gaze upon the bright stars. Oddly, the night air was often cool and this star gazing reminded me of those cool summer nights in up-state New York where I spent my childhood.

After dinner I planned to work on some paperwork but I didn't want to think about it now. I just wanted to have a relaxing drive.

Just as I stopped at a traffic light, I received a call from my brother blurting out that he just read a very short announcement on-line … Bernard Madoff was arrested! Arrested for what?

I do not remember the rest of my ride.

When I arrived home, the first thing I did was go on-line in search of any information about Bernard Madoff's arrest.

From that moment I knew my life would never be the same. Losing my Florida home and living in cold New Jersey immediately came into my thoughts. Then I thought of all the years I had worked hard to earn a living and save for the future; and then I thought of my investment with Madoff. This was some reward for all my years of work. What was I going to live on? And what about my family ... my siblings and parents had invested in Madoff, and now their life savings were gone too.

December 11, 2009 has come and gone; a year has passed since that call from my brother.

Early on, I had sold some of my household items, and, not knowing what else I should do I put other possessions in long term storage, and then left Florida in early 2009. The best plan seemed to be to move back to New Jersey and live with my sister where we could consolidate our expenses. This Madoff mess triggered a series of changes, big and small.

No more health club, no more Sunday drive to nowhere, no more hairdresser, and no more time to do the volunteer work I used to enjoy. During this past year, I have gone out to dinner only twice; gone to the movies only twice ... both of these occasions were to celebrate birthdays. Broadway and local theater is but a distant memory of a by-gone era. I haven't played golf since leaving Florida.

My plans for retirement must be put off indefinitely. All the saving and planning were useless.

The work ethic which my parents cultivated during my childhood galvanized in engineering college. They formed the foundation for my conservative life style and spending habits. Yet here I am taking steps to strip my spending down to bare bones. What an irony.

I worked up a budget and kept to it, and continually referred to it, to see if there were any other costs I could trim. I worked hard to pay my bills and keep the excellent credit rating I always had. If there was one thing I wanted to protect, it was my credit rating. Imagine my shock when I received a letter from the firm that was working on the liquidation of the Madoff mess. This firm informed me in September 2009 that a laptop containing many Madoff victims' (including my) personal and confidential information had been stolen from the car of one of their staff. Wow! What next?

This reminded me of the days shortly following the Madoff arrest when the name and address of all the victims who had directly invested with Madoff were published on-line and in the newspaper. This seemed like such an invasion of privacy. I received many unsolicited letters from insurance companies, investment firms and law firms inquiring as to whether they could be of service to me in my time of need. All unwelcome junk mail!

It's been well over a year since Madoff was arrested, and I still have not received any money that I should have received based on the formula established by the Securities Investor Protection Corp. Trustee (who is liquidating the Madoff mess). This is surely a test of patience and will. The uncertainty of the future certainly creates tension. All my life I played by the rules, and now there is no playbook.

So far I've only mentioned the small things in life that have changed, except, of course making the big move up north. On the plus side, I have been able to spend more time with my family that live in New Jersey.

This has been a blessing.

I have also experienced over the course of the year some small, but memorable, acts of kindness from family, friends, professional colleagues, and other Madoff victims I've met on-line in support- and advocacy-groups. Simple pleasures such as sharing lunch with a friend and being treated to a relaxing game of golf were so helpful to lift my spirit.

I will always remember the day I learned of Madoff's arrest; I will always remember the year that followed when I learned of the SEC's repeated failures to stop the Madoff fraud and the SIPC failure to fulfill its obligations to make prompt payments to innocent victims.   I've survived the year, but where will I be five, ten years from now?   Will I be OK?   How will my family fare? Those chapters in my life have yet to be written.

Reflecting back on this whole experience, one lesson I have learned is that it's probably better to spend for today and not worry about tomorrow.

I'll always remember where I was the day President Kennedy was shot. I'll always remember where I was and what I was doing when Neil Armstrong and Buzz Aldrin landed on the moon and I'll always remember Thursday December 11, 2008

I never was an early riser. I'm an owl. I stay up late and get up early if I have to. I was up and playing golf with my regular Thursday group by 7:44 a.m. My favorite part of the day is joining the group for lunch. I do remember saying how "sick" I was of going out for dinner all the time, but social life in Florida revolves around dinner dates.

I said my husband was going to kill me for making another date and I was hoping the couple would cancel when of course she came right up to me and confirmed our date.

At 5:00 p.m. that evening our son-in-law called to tell us Bernie Madoff was arrested. We had no other information. We were quite in shock I guess, and went to a very casual pizza place with a television.

My friend asked "What are you watching over my shoulder?"

I said "Look at the screen, Madoff was arrested."

She was gleeful! She knew a lot of people who were invested. Then we told her we were wiped out. EVERYTHING; all my husband and I had in the world was the money in our checking account and our social security payments.

I knew almost immediately that life as I knew it was over.

I just exhaled and I've been like that ever since.

Hardship creates strong coping skills.

I was born to a poor Jewish family, the second girl. My mother told my sister and I that pretty girls were a dime a dozen and we had to be good students; we had to be smart. We never went to camp; summers were spent at the public beach in Coney Island. My sister and I shared one used bicycle, we never owned a car, the encyclopedia, or rode in taxies. We took the subway to free museums, walked to the library and had the cheapest seats at the Metropolitan Opera house.

We lived two flights above a store in Coney Island. Then we moved to a middle class neighborhood with better schools but we were still two flights above a store. I walked to school and later took a bus to a City College; the registration fee per semester was $28. Like most women of my generation I was told that my true career would be wife and mother. Marriage was going to be my path to a different life.

I married the man my mother always wanted me to and had a son. We were divorced ten years when he died in his sleep. I had to tell my son his father was dead. I married the man I always wanted to and we saved to have a down payment for a house. We moved to the suburbs; at last I had my house and I was active in school and community charities. Along with Betty Freidan, Gloria Steinem, *Ms Magazine*, burning bras, equitable distribution, the sex revolution, it was the turbulent 60's and 70's and I wanted to work. I had enough of volunteering.

I worked in Manhattan in the garment center and commuted with my husband. I was doing well and we thought it would be a good time for him to start a business of his own. Unfortunately that business soon failed. I became the sole support of the family when my second husband had a mental breakdown and was later murdered by a drug dealer. I had to tell my daughter her father was dead.

My third husband was a widower and Holocaust survivor who struggled to raise two of his own children and build a business.

I pooled what was left of my money and we bought a house. He died in 1986 after a five year battle with cancer; leaving me the house, $200,000 and a car. I had to watch the person I love suffer and die. I worked in town in a boutique. I managed to pay my bills and my taxes. I looked after my children, my mother and my grandchildren when they arrived.

I've volunteered my time and services in whatever community I lived in and continue to do so.

In 1996 my then-fiancé had his IRA with Madoff and spoke on my behalf to a money manager who said I didn't have enough money to "get in" but it was close enough. I should open an account with Cohmad Securities Corp. (1996) and when I sold my house I could transfer the additional money to Bernard L Madoff Investment Securities (December 16, 1996) He said he would "take me" and they sure did.

That is how Bernard L Madoff Investment Securities came to have all the money that I had in the world. Was it safe? Of course, my fiancé said. He was with him for years and Madoff was investigated by and sanctioned by the SEC in 1992. His IRA was totally invested in Madoff. The IRS sanctioned BMIS to be an IRA Custodian. Of course it was safe.

I don't have the luxury of dwelling on how this came to pass. I can't expend energy thinking of Bernie Madoff and what could motivate a man to do what he did. I can't think of Ruthie, or Peter or the rest of the family; the custodian of the IRA, the insiders or the advisor I knew for 35 years who "got me into" Madoff. I can't wonder why the SEC wasn't doing what they were paid to do.

188

I didn't do anything wrong. I paid my taxes with real money on phantom income. My Medicare D payments are configured on phantom income and can't be readjusted until 2010. I'm paying a surcharge for the taxes that were paid on money that wasn't there.

After a lifetime of being dependable and responsible **all** the money that I have in the world is gone. It only took an instant to learn we were catapulted into poverty. That's life changing.

Trouble is a great teacher. I've learned a lot in the last year.

I've learned that you can't do it alone and you have to let family and good friends who step forward help with emotional support.

I've learned this really is the perfect storm. I can't make my mortgage payments and I can't find a buyer for my house. I can't find work in the midst of a great recession. I can't roll back the clock and become 40 once again.

I've learned I have to reinvent myself at 68. I'm going to have to find something I can do for the next 25 years.

I've learned that there are no guarantees.

I learned it's not how much money you lost its how much money you have left.

My husband is 78 years old. He didn't waste any time. He went to work doing telephone customer sales. He worked from 7:30 a.m. until 8:30 p.m. six days a week for commission only. He was terminated after three months because he did not make the quota of sales they projected. He is now trying to do hosting at a local bagel store.

My mother is 94 years old. I have always paid part of her long term care insurance in addition to supplementing her income. My mother does not know about the change in my circumstances and I hope she never finds out. We have eleven grandchildren; you can imagine checks for birthdays and holidays. We have always given. I think that is the hardest thing of all. It's bad enough that we can't give anymore; we now have to go to our children and siblings for money to just get by.

How long can you do that? It's one thing to help out but no one in our family is able to support us.

Madoff investors are victims of a catastrophic event. The media is fascinated by the glamorous lifestyle the Madoffs indulged in. It's the wrong story.

When is someone going to wake up and realize that the whole financial system is at risk? Why doesn't the average investor see that they could lose their securities to a thief and SIPC will not pay them? Why does the government (Congress) allow SIPC to continue to advertise protection when they don't have the funds to do so?

The government agencies which we depended upon to safeguard us have failed. The financial insurance provided by SIPC to protect the investor is really protecting the brokers. Why isn't there a public outcry when the trustee's lawyers are being paid $1 million a week by SIPC and the SEC testified that SIPC can't pay the victims? Why is the president of the SIPC allowed to run an under funded insurance agency, when AIG wasn't? The trustee anticipates litigation, because he's not following the statute as written; but like the Holocaust survivors before us, we won't be alive to see restitution and if we are, the process is only adding to our hardship.

I exhale.

I took steps all my life so that I would not end up the way I began; poor, and here I am. How am I going to live the rest of my life? How do I live old and poor in America? I'd rather not think.

I've spent the year fulfilling family and community obligations. I've spent the year reading e-mails from my Madoff support groups; writing to Senators and Congressman; filling out SIPC claim forms with gratis legal help, working on amending tax returns and trying to get our Social Security and Medicare payments adjusted.

I guess I think something will work out after all; it always does. Nothing ever stays the same; the good things or the bad.

It's time to get to work and earn money. I'm going back to school and join the army of Florida real estate professionals. If I can't sell my own house who will?

So many people tell me I'm a survivor; perhaps it's because I always bounce back. My husband always said I was a pessimist but I always answered, "with my life experience I'm a realist." I don't take anything for granted, I had a good run; what goes up comes down. I'll have to hope it goes up again.

When my daughter cried for me I told her not to shed a tear. I've suffered great loss in my life many times. Real loss; and I can say honestly that it's the people in your life that are irreplaceable. We were financially devastated and traumatized by Madoff's Ponzi scheme but the one event that brought me to my knees this year was the death of my daughter-in-laws only 21 year old son to a motorcycle accident. I'm grateful that we have our health, we have each other, we have loving family and friends and we have hope that we can find a way to be financially independent again.

N.E.S. - Still Standing.

Interesting Life Is Overrated
Alexandra Roth

Happy and uneventful would describe our family's life until the afternoon of December 11th, 2008, when out of a blissful obscurity, we got sucked into the fraud of the century. We were the average American family, married, two kids, one house, one dog, two cars, living on a quiet street in a small town in New Jersey. We, and thousands of other victims, had done nothing wrong, and yet, our names, addresses and financial life story was made public all over the country and the world. We had no say in it, nor were there any attempts made to consider the consequences of such a massive release of information on the innocent victims.

We were the subject of ridicule and scorn, and we could only stand by and watch as newspaper after newspaper, commentator after commentator, kept blaming the victims for the tragedy that befell them. Gradually though, this perception by the media and the public started to change, as more victims of the fraud came forward and spoke out in their own defense, and even traveled all the way to Congress to present their case.

Now, a year later, our family is picking up the pieces of what was once a good and happy life and trying to fit them into a new reality.

We were the typical middle class family, with a simple life plan: work hard, buy a house, send kids to college, retire and enjoy your retirement years. With some bumps in life's road, health issues mainly, we almost made it to the retirement part, when our life was turned upside down with the revelation of the Madoff fraud.

We had never heard of Madoff until after we had already been invested with him for many years. The investment was made upon a recommendation from a relative. Madoff had an excellent reputation and a track record that was considered the envy of Wall Street. We felt secure in knowing he had been investing our relative's money for many years with good results.

Our reaction to the news of the fraud was total shock and disbelief. The first thing that came to my mind was," it must be a terrible mistake". Then it became quickly very clear that we were the victims of a huge Ponzi scheme. But, being a Registered Representative with the NASD (the predecessor of FINRA) for many years, I knew (so I thought) that our investment was protected by SIPC, and therefore not all was lost. That belief was also short lived as it was dispelled by SIPC in short order.

The SIPC's position of refusing to pay victims "promptly" based on their last statement, turned out to be our biggest shock and surprise in this whole fraud story. Yes, fraud happens, but this time, we felt we were being defrauded by the agencies that were supposed to protect us.

Like many investors, we believed that SIPC protects the investor of a failed broker/dealer, no matter how the fraud was comitted. If you check the SIPC website it does not say that in case of a Ponzi scheme there is no coverage, or that a Ponzi scheme calls for a forensic accounting investigation, or that an innocent Ponzi scheme victim is actually considered a thief and lastly that a Ponzi scheme investigation may last ten years or longer. None of that. Yet, the SIPC is using all those points as roadblocks to prevent the victims of this fraud from collecting what the SIPC owes them. SIPC has adopted this strategy for one reason only: to avoid paying the claims as the SIPA (Securities Investor Protection Act) law mandates. The SIPA law states that the claims should be paid "promptly" based on the last customer statement.

Why is SIPC refusing to pay the claims? The simple truth, which they refuse to admit, is that they were caught under funded. One doesn't have to be a rocket scientist to figure out that if a broker/dealer pays $150 per year, not a month, for 19 years, for a coverage of up to $500,000 that it would not be enough to fill the reserves in case of a large financial fraud or failure. For all intents and purposes the SIPC is bankrupt. Not only does SIPC lack the funds to pay current investors who were defrauded, (Mary Schapiro, SEC Chairwoman, admitted to this before Congress) if another large financial firm goes under in the near future - and that is not inconceivable - the SIPC's reserves will not be sufficient to make good on its promise. Yet again. Right now the only people benefiting from the existence of SIPC are Stephen Harbeck the CEO and the employees of SIPC; and of course Irving Picard, the court appointed trustee for the liquidation of Madoff's assets. Congress should order that the SIPC be closed down until they can justify their existence to the investors.

SIPC's positions should be of great concern to all investors since no one can predict how a fraud will be committed. Based on our experience, SIPC cannot be relied upon to deliver on their stated mission. The SIPC Mission as stated on their official website http://www.sipc.org/who/sipcmission.cfm reads:

"When a brokerage firm is closed due to bankruptcy or other financial difficulties and customer assets are missing, SIPC steps in as quickly as possible and, within certain limits, works to return customers' cash, stock and other securities. Without SIPC, investors at financially troubled brokerage firms might lose their securities or money forever or wait for years while their assets are tied up in court. Although not every investor is protected by SIPC, no fewer than 99 percent of persons who are eligible get their investments back from SIPC. From its creation by Congress in 1970 through December 2008, SIPC advanced $520 million in order to make possible the recovery of $160 billion in assets for an estimated 761,000 investors."

"SIPC steps in as quickly as possible"? It has been over a year now and we have not heard from SIPC. Madoff's firm had SIPC coverage, and yet we are being treated as though he had no coverage: "Without SIPC, investors at financially troubled brokerage firms might lose their securities or money forever or wait for years while their assets are tied up in court." What is the point of having SIPC coverage?

For nineteen years SIPC members paid $150 a year for the privilege of using the designation of "Member SIPC" on their statements. Imagine a company like Goldman Sachs, Merrill Lynch, and JP Morgan –billion dollar companies – paying $150 a year, not a month! At some point, the SIPC was warned by Congress that their reserves might not be enough to meet large financial failures, but they chose not to act on those warnings. They changed the fees only after the Madoff fraud, by which time thousands of innocent investors were left with nothing.

SIPC is governed by SIPA (Securities Investor Protection Act) law, and as intended by Congress, SIPC was meant to protect the "Reasonable Expectations" of the investor. And that means, the investor expects that the statements he/she gets from the broker/dealer, such as Merrill Lynch for example, are real and he/she is entitled to the returns as shown on these statements. The SIPC decided that because it was a Ponzi scheme, the investor is not entitled to the returns. So the question is, how does an average investor know in advance that he/she is invested with a Ponzi scheme? Contrary to what the SIPC wants you to believe, the average investor lacks the resources and knowledge to identify this type of fraud.

We have come to the unavoidable conclusion, that there is no one looking out for the interests of the small/average investor. Not the SEC, not SIPC, not FINRA, no one. In fact they try to protect themselves from the investors. Their strategy comes down to putting the blame on the investors themselves. Blame the victim strategy. Only this time, the SEC's own Inspector General Kotz's report pulls the rug completely from under their lame argument. Every investor in America should go to the SEC website (address

195

provided in the Glossary section) and read the report. You will be shocked by the revelations in this report. In fact, if enough Americans read this report, there will be a run on sleeping aids in this country, when they learn how incompetent and mismanaged the SEC was found to be.

Why have so few in the government suffered any consequnces as a result of this disaster? Take the SEC for example; they were found sleeping at the switch when the largest Ponzi scheme happened right under their nose. They had ample evidence thrown in their face, but they refused to act on it because it would have been " time consuming" as per the Inspector General Kotz's report. $65 billion later, the time they saved by not investigating, cost investors billions of dollars. Thousands of lives were destroyed, and one would think after such a major blunder we'd see major firings of those responsible. That didn't happen. There were some who left voluntarily, but there was nothing on the scale that would match the devastation they caused by their incompetence.

While the SEC employees had not time to investigate Madoff, seems they had plenty of time to surf the Internet, for hours on end, looking at porn, at taxpayer's expense! On government provided computers! It has been reported that some engaged in this behavior for eight hours a day for five years. Imagine what they could have accomplished during that time had they chosen instead to do their job. How unfortunate and tragic for thousands of victims, if some of those senior and highly paid employees that have engaged in this behavior, also made the decision not to investigate Madoff. Those employees should have been fired, but they were not. Most were only disciplined. Where is justice, SEC?

Though the investigation of the fraud itself by the authorities is still unwinding, there has been little progress made by the government agencies responsible, in addressing the concerns and issues resulting from this unprecedented Ponzi scheme. The little progress that has been made was due to pressure from the victims groups, not due to government's own initiative.

196

My advice to you is not to invest in the market because you can never tell if you are invested in a Ponzi scheme, no matter how smart you, or your advisors are. Though you will get lower returns, you are better off putting your money in the bank, where at least you are guaranteed your returns and your initial investment. It is worth the peace of mind knowing that your money is really protected, unlike with the SIPC, where the promise has been proven to be hollow. With SIPC, if you happened innocently to take out more money than you put in - because you thought the money was there and you had statements proving it to you- the SIPC will demand that money back, along with your initial investment. The SIPC will not recognize your earnings even though you had planned your life around it and made financial decisions based on those statements, and in spite of the fact that they are supposed to honor the last statement you receive from your broker/dealer. I hope you learn from our mistake and next time you see the logo "Member SIPC", run the other way because the logo is meaningless, and it can actually hurt your financial future. You might be wise also to contact your Representatives in Congress and voice your concerns and demand they wake up and act to protect the small investor.

We have been adjusting to our new life and moving forward. Of course it has not been easy, and every day has some reminders of life past. Gone are the common" luxuries" typical of a middle class life: travel, eating out, giving to charity; these are no longer a part of our lives. Helping our daughter with her future wedding plans will no longer be possible, unless things change. Gift giving during the holidays will always be a reminder of things past. Being an avid cook and baker, I no longer have the budget for this little luxury. The worst is we have to sell our house, a home we have lived in for almost 32 years.

In short, life is much simpler now. We draw comfort from seeing our kids do well and lead happy and productive lives in spite of what has happened. We also draw strength from each other, and keep looking to the future with a curious excitement that seems misplaced, but is real. It feels like an adventure, starting over at an age when most people plan on retiring. Actually, it is an adventure, and it has energized us and made us feel young again. *So this is the formula for staying young.* We'd like to share this formula with the world, but we doubt we'll find any takers; the price might be an impediment.

We were winding down our careers, my husband in the computer field, and I in the insurance field. Going back to work past one's prime is a daunting challenge anytime, but in today's economy it is doubly so. However, we are not discouraged; we are actually excited and ready to take on this challenge and keep going forward for as long as we can. It is our new reality. Our hearts, though, go out to those victims who can no longer, for age or health reasons, take on any challenge to support themselves. This is the real tragedy.

A disaster of this magnitude is very humbling, but it has taught us certain things about ourselves, that have enriched our lives already. After being independent for all of our adult lives, accepting help from our children has been the most humbling of experiences. It is beyond heartwarming to see what wonderful human beings we have contributed to this world. It is without a doubt, the biggest legacy of our lives.

Traumatic events like these also test our strength and resolve. I found strength I never thought I had; I found new vigor and meaning in the pursuit of justice, by joining forces with other victims and pursuing legislation that will help prevent future frauds of this type, while better protecting victims' rights.

There are really no solutions to prevent this from happening again. Not even the government with the best of intentions and laws can prevent it, but it can ameliorate the situation when it happens. Furthermore, it is also unrealistic to expect the average investors to completely protect themselves from fraud. To the extent that is possible to protect the investors, we have our various government agencies whose job it is to be the "firewall" between the crooks and the innocent investors. When these agencies fail, the ultimate victims are always the small/average investors. That is why we, the victims of this fraud, have made it our mission to demand reform and accountability from our government.

Throughout the struggle for our cause, we have found great comfort in an online support community that was created by the victims. We were a group of strangers whose lives were devastated by this fraud, who in the end turned into a virtual family, supporting and encouraging each other's efforts. Though at first our mood was depressed and our spirits low, with every piece of good news and small victories our mood became more positive as we dared to hope. We now fit the ultimate definition of an optimist: "Someone who goes after Moby Dick in a row boat, and brings tartar sauce with him". We have many battles still ahead, but we have plenty of tartar sauce on board.

As to our family, we now live a different life from previous years, maybe even an interesting life, but not by choice. From where we stand now, our previous uneventful life would have been our choice, but life presents the unexpected sometimes, with disastrous results, and it's up to us to make sense of it and keep on moving. At this point we still feel as though we are getting off a roller coaster ride, we are still a bit dizzy from the ride, and feel shaky on our feet. But, we hope this year our head will finally stop spinning and return to a state of stability and calm, and with it we'll be able to welcome peace back into our lives.

March 18 2010

BERNARD L. MADOFF
INMATE # 61727-054
FCI BUTNER MEDIUM I
FEDERAL CORRECTIONAL INSTITUTION
P.O. BOX 1000
BUTNER, NC 27509

Hello Bernie!

One hell of a ride, huh? Did you ever think it would last as long as it did? Those regulators, what a bunch of Hoopleheads. They couldn't find their asses using both hands with the lights on!

I know you've been busy with all of the legal entanglements and so on, and then settling in there at Butner, that can't be easy. Let me fill you in on some of the news, in case you don't have broadband yet.

They appointed Mary Schapiro as Chairwoman of the Securities and Exchange Commission after her tenure at Financial Industry Regulatory Authority worked out so well. So well in fact, that just weeks after your confession they gave her a 7 million dollar severance package. There's Something About Mary.

Bernie, you can't make stuff like this up - She fails to detect your fraud for 16 years at FINRA and its predecessor NASD so they appoint her to head of the SEC which also failed to detect your fraud even after they were given the play book by Harry Markopolos. They appoint Mary, who did not discover your fraud and don't appoint Harry that did discover your fraud. All I am saying here is that opportunities still abound.

Wasn't it back in 2001 that she appointed your son, Mark to serve on the board of the National Adjudicatory Council – the division

201

that reviews disciplinary decisions made by FINRA? That kind of forward thinking is indeed impressive.

Then there is SIPC: they think they have found a methodology to only pay a small fraction of the claims! These guys are good and talent like that does not go unrewarded. They are spending $1 million per week on forensic accounting and $1 million per week on attorney's fees and SIPC is footing the bill. At this rate in 5 years they'll have spent $500 million but will have saved SIPC and Wall Street $2.5 billion! All without the possibility of criminal sanctions! Like I said, Bernie, these guys are real good.

Just 47,361 days to go! Keep the dauber up. Things can turn around in an instant and you could be right back on top again and Mary has that $7 million severance package that needs money managing.

Regards,
Tim Murray

BERNARD L. MADOFF
INMATE # 61727-054
FCI BUTNER MEDIUM I
FEDERAL CORRECTIONAL INSTITUTION
P.O. BOX 1000
BUTNER, NC 27509

Mr. Madoff,

You are a monster.

What part of your soul is missing that has made you become one of the most hated men in history? Do you have a soul?

You have ravaged widows, like me, charities and innocent people from all over the world. You have cunningly plundered us all, leaving us impoverished and destroyed our dreams of leaving our children a better life.

Did you not receive enough love as you grew up? Or, did the family you grew up in teach you that greed and stealing was the path to achieve your goals of an excessive, extravagant, and filthy rich life style?

You stole my life's savings. I don't have enough life left to ever come close to recovering what you cold heartedly stole from me.

My husband and I WORKED our entire lives for what we accumulated. You stole your entire life for what you accumulated.

My husband got up in the middle of the night, year after year, to drive to the hospital in snow, sleet, hail, wind and ice to save someone's precious life. Did he do that throughout his too short life so that you could buy another piece of meaningless jewelry for your wife?

You are an evil predator. You need to be locked away forever. I wish that there could be a non-stop tape playing in your cell of all the victims' faces and voices. We would tell you what it feels like to get that call that said everything we had worked for, everything we had wanted to leave behind to charities and families, and the future we had dreamed about, was stolen.

I was left with what was in my wallet and what was in my checking account.

You did not destroy my faith in humanity because I have received so much generosity and kindness from so many. I became poor, and at the same time, I became rich in the knowledge of people's goodness. In the future I will "pay it forward" as a tribute to the people who have helped me .

I was in the court room when one of my fellow victims told you of the legacy you leave to your family. Instead of pride and honor of bearing the name Madoff, they will be reviled and despised and bear the shame of your abominable deeds. That is what you leave behind for your descendents.

The Bible says that as Christ hung on the cross He cried out to God, "Father forgive them, for they know not what they do." I do not forgive you. You and your family knew exactly what you were doing. You will face God soon, and he will hold you accountable for your sins.

Maureen Ebel

July 23, 2009

Inmate Mail/Parcels
Mr. Bernard Madoff (Prisoner # 61727-054)
BUTNER MEDIUM I FCI
P.O. BOX 1000
BUTNER NC 27509

Dear Mr. Madoff:

I am one of the many thousands of Americans that trusted you with their financial future. In 1992 I took money saved over the first 20 years of my working life and gave all of that to BMIS. Over the next 10 years I added to my investments on a regular basis. My retirement date was set at February of 2010 and that would also be the beginning of my withdrawals from this long term investment vehicle. Needless to say, that retirement date has been indefinitely postponed and will likely never occur.

This letter is not targeted towards attributing responsibility for this financial catastrophe to your actions, but to offer you a means of perhaps atoning for the damage that you have done to so many. Forgiveness or absolution is asking too much of those who have lost their family fortunes, financial freedom and retirement lifestyle. But perhaps you can still do something to return part of those lost assets by telling your story to one who is prepared to listen. I have the unique position to be one of those who lost much to your deceit. I attended your sentencing in New York and was partially satisfied by the lifetime sentence pronounced by the judge. That part of my life is over. Now the next phase begins. Most of my life in now focused on addressing our government to return taxes paid on falsified 1099s.

You have played the role of the good soldier by protecting all others from being implicated. I assume that you will continue to

205

take that position. Therefore, if you do decide to tell part of your story I presume that it will focus on how you did it and how you induced the regulatory agencies to "look the other way." Information on that process would be of great value to your investors. It may even help you and the treatment of your family because you would be viewed as having some compassion for those who lost so much. It may be the only thing that you can ever do to assist with restitution. There may be other topics you would like to talk about. Again, I am prepared to listen.

Bernie, I hope that you take this letter to heart and view it as a means of doing something to rescue your eternal soul and demonstrate that you are not the monster that many have made you out to be.

Michael De Vita

BERNARD L. MADOFF
Inmate # 61727-054
FCI BUTNER MEDIUM I
FEDERAL CORRECTIONAL INSTITUTION
P.O. BOX 1000
BUTNER, NC 27509

There was a time when I hated you.

There was a time when I wanted nothing more than to see you and your family suffer.

But, today, I say thank you.

Thank you for taking me to the edge of insanity, because it was then, and only then, that I realized I had the courage and inner strength to stop myself from falling. It was then, and only then, that I knew what it truly meant to hate. But, I realized that if I had that much anger, resentment and hate inside of me, I could only imagine how much love I have inside that I have not yet begun to share.

It was then, and only then, that I no longer dreamt or wished for you to suffer, because I realized that if one person can cause so much pain to so many people, then the opposite must be true, and one person can give just as much joy to just as many people.

It was during those lonely nights and days when I contemplated ending it all, all of the madness created by you, that somewhere, somehow, I discovered a place which I never knew existed, a place where there was so much courage, so much strength, a place where life is precious, and you learn to treasure every moment. Because, that is what life is, a succession of moments that make up years-months-weeks-days-hours-minutes-and seconds. To have discovered such a place within me has been priceless.

I no longer stand on the edge of insanity, waiting for that final push. The days and nights are no longer dark and lonely, but instead are filled with joy and hope and happiness that brighten my every moment.

I no longer hate you. You are no longer the Monster that terrifies my dreams and fills my nightmares, because now I have courage and strength, and I have taken back control of my life.

This ordeal has allowed me to grow. It has allowed me to be a better friend, a better daughter, a better sister, a better me.

And for that I say, thank you!

AKL

BERNARD L. MADOFF
Inmate # 61727-054
FCI BUTNER MEDIUM I
FEDERAL CORRECTIONAL INSTITUTION
P.O. BOX 1000
BUTNER, NC 27509

madoff:

I have a few questions to ask you which I am sure you have been asked already, either by your family, or now, by your esteemed neighbors in your new "gated" retirement community: WAS IT REALLY WORTH IT? Looking back now, would you have done it again? By the way, how are you managing without your forty Rolex watches, your thousand count sheets, your five thousand dollars suits, and your countless fancy shoes? How is life without your American Express card backed by your "loyal" victims? We can arrange for an extra hot dog for you, if you tell us where you hid the money and who helped you.

I have heard that some members of your immediate family are looking to change their last names. Your grandchildren will no longer carry your last name either. There is no worse rejection, don't you agree? After all, you did it for them, didn't you? To make them proud, to show them and the world what a genius you were; to leave a legacy for the history books. You sure did. But it's a legacy your family will try to run away from for as long as they live. You left them a legacy of an evil genius, a genius who has no soul, no conscience and is completely devoid of morals and humanity; a shell of a human being. Is that how you want to go and meet your maker? You can still do something to change that.

And you know that your family will be hounded for years to come, even with the new names. They will have no peace, until you die, and then until they die. What a horrible fate for your innocent grandchildren to bear; that their grandfather was the worst financial criminal in history. How will they look at the family pictures and remember you? Will they look with disgust? Pain? Shame? Will they look at all? Will they destroy them so they can forget you sooner? You brought eternal shame on all your future descendants. Wherever they live, they will hide this secret and live with it in shame. You even put Ponzi to shame, and it's no longer a Ponzi scheme, it's a madoff scheme. What a horrible way to live on.

Do you think your family members would have taken this drastic step of changing their last name, had you come out and assisted the government in finding and recovering the money and shown remorse? Who helped you? Why are you not speaking and cooperating now? Do it at least to find a measure of peace for yourself, but more importantly of course, to help restore victims' lives. Granted, your life is ruined, but with your answers you can still help the innocent victims. It is never too late to do the right thing, madoff.

Your family wants nothing to do with you. Humanity wants nothing to do with you. Is this a way to leave this world, with such extreme and utter rejection by everyone on this planet? Your name and deeds are forever going to be remembered as the greatest financial evil perpetrated by a single human being. Still, you can do something to show your family and the victims that you've tried to atone. It might even get you a better "seat" in hell.

So many questions, so little time, for you that is, and that's a shame. You know, locking you up without getting the answers from you was the biggest mistake our government had made; how can we prevent this from happening again if we don't learn from the grand master of thievery himself - that is you- how this transpired? Where is the money? That is where you can still help. It's not too late, madoff.

Who in the government helped you? Turned a blind eye? Who got bribed by you? This would be of enormous help to us as a society to know in order to clean up the system and help prevent other future scams. You have caused a horrific financial disaster to thousands of innocent people but you can still make up for it in a small way by helping us strengthen our financial system, so that in the future even your grandchildren will benefit.

Well genius, you were just a thief. A plain thief. I bet, a blindfolded monkey throwing darts at a board would have picked stocks better than you. Anyone could pick stocks better than you. You just knew how to steal better than anyone; ever.

Does it make you feel proud? Do you think about it while sitting in your tiny cell, with that wonderful aroma of urine permeating your lungs, or while waiting for that one miserable hour when you get to go outside and see a tiny sliver of the sky? Do you think about it while dining on bologna sandwiches? And if you do think about it, do you have any regrets, madoff?

If you want to leave this world a better place, (and just for the sake of your family, why wouldn't you?) give us some answers. Tell us, how did you do it? Where have you hidden the money? Why not help and answer these questions? Why not root out the evil you sowed?

madoff, it's not too late. Do the right thing, ex-master of the universe.

Alexandra Roth – Poor for now, but free as a bird forever!

P.S. I have been spelling your name in low caps for a while now, simply because you are a low life.

BERNARD L. MADOFF
Inmate # 61727-054
FCI BUTNER MEDIUM I
FEDERAL CORRECTIONAL INSTITUTION
P.O. BOX 1000
BUTNER, NC 27509

Mr. Madoff,

I never met you, yet you had more influence and control over my life than I ever did. I guess that in your quest for unlimited money you did not think of the consequences that would be endured by your investors. If one wish were granted to me I would wish that you would tell the truth about everything that happened inside your investment business. We, the victims, desperately need to have some of our money refunded so that we may go on with our lives. We did nothing to harm you and now we need your help. Whatever you did, you did. But you still have time to redeem yourself by cooperating with the authorities to help us now in our time of need. The government is not protecting us. You are the only one to whom we may turn for help.

Sincerely,
Stephanie Halio

BERNARD L. MADOFF
Inmate # 61727-054
FCI BUTNER MEDIUM I
FEDERAL CORRECTIONAL INSTITUTION
P.O. BOX 1000
BUTNER, NC 27509

Mister Madoff,

Why don't you explain?

What really happened?

What's in your sick brain?

A guilty plea …a conspiracy!

With your cronies and your family!

And what about The SEC?

Lock him up in solitary!

Bernie… where the hell is all the money?

Regrets,
Norma Human

P.S. American Dream…A Ponzi Scheme…Blown up in smoke…
Madoff in America…Now everyone's broke…

(From the YOUTUBE video): "MADOFF IN AMERICA"
(An Original Rap-Disco Drama)

Analysis: Madoff's Returns vs. The Market
Michael De Vita

Should The Madoff Rate Of Return Have Made Investors Suspicious?

Who is to blame for the Madoff fraud? Is it the SEC for failing to discover the Ponzi scheme despite repeated investigations? How about the IRS for approving Madoff to handle IRA and pension money? Could it be the employees of Madoff's firm who were exposed to the daily activities of the fraud and yet claim to be totally surprised? Perhaps it was the feeder fund managers who collected large fees while failing to oversee Bernard Madoff's investments. Or is it the individual investors who accepted Madoff as an investment manager for many years?

Most likely, all bear some varying degree of responsibility. Since this book focuses on the individual stories of a number of Madoff investors, this chapter will address the issue of investor responsibility for judging the reasonableness of the returns on their investment accounts.

Madoff investors have been criticized for accepting returns that were reported in the press as being well above those that the average investor would expect to receive by investing in the stock market.

Indeed, a "blame the victim" mentality has been pervasive in the press and many have commented that Madoff investors should have known that the returns reported on their accounts were "too good to be true."

As has been reported by Irving Picard (the trustee handling the bankruptcy) there were two classes of Madoff accounts. Out of almost 5,000 active Madoff accounts there were 245 special accounts that belonged to family members and special friends such

214

as Stanley Chais, Jeffry Picower and others that had a long-standing relationship with Madoff. These special accounts received return rates that were far in excess of those that were reported for the majority of Madoff investors.

Many Madoff investors report that the average return to those 4,755 "non-special" accounts was about 10% to 11% per annum. A number of investors stated that it was not the rate of return that attracted them to invest with Madoff, but rather Madoff's statement that his split-strike conversion strategy generated consistency and predictability with neither large gains nor large losses. While the market can generate large single year gains (the S&P increased 23.5% in 2009 and the NASDAQ increased 44%) Madoff investors would never see such large gains nor would their accounts suffer large losses.

Is An 11% Annual Return Unreasonable?

In order to address the reasonableness of an 11% annual return it is necessary to compare this to the returns an investor would receive from large mutual fund companies that invest in stocks. Four large mutual fund companies that have individual funds with long term track records were selected as the basis for comparison. The four fund companies include: The American Mutual Fund Company, Fidelity Mutual Funds, Janus Mutual Funds and Vanguard Mutual funds. Within each mutual fund company four individual mutual funds were evaluated. Since Madoff perpetrated his fraud over decades, only funds that have been in business for an extended period were selected. The returns for the selected mutual funds were reported on the Vanguard.com web site in November of 2009.

Madoff Returns versus American Mutual Fund Company

Four American Funds were selected for comparison. These four funds were started from 1934 to 1978 and include Growth Fund of America (1978), Fundamental (1978), Investment Company of American (1934) and American Mutual (1950). The chart below shows the average annual return reported by Madoff was actually lower than that for all four American Funds. With the exception of the Growth Fund of American, Madoff's return was within one percentage point of the other three funds.

American Mutual Funds
Average Annual Return

Returns reported on Vanguard.com website, November 2009

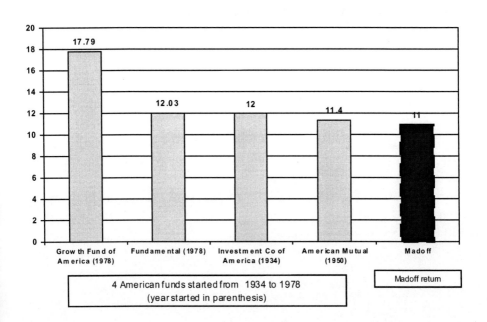

Madoff Returns Versus Fidelity Mutual Funds.

Four Fidelity Funds were selected for comparison. These four funds were started from 1963 to 1985 and include Magellan (1963), Advisor Diversified Stock (1970), Growth (1983) and Advisor Capital Development (1985). The same pattern as observed for American Funds appears for the Fidelity comparison. Madoff's reported annual return was lower than any of these four long-term funds. Again, Madoff's return was within one and a half percentage points of three of the funds. Magellan fund greatly outperformed all three Fidelity funds as well as Madoff.

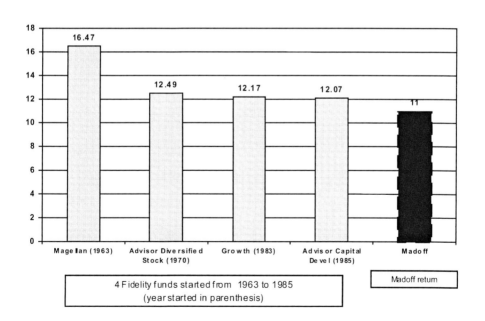

Fidelity Mutual Funds
Average Annual Return

Returns reported on Vanguard.com website, November 2009

4 Fidelity funds started from 1963 to 1985 (year started in parenthesis)

Madoff return

Madoff Returns Versus Janus Mutual Funds.

Four Janus Funds were selected for comparison. These four funds were started from 1970 to 1998 and include Small Cap Value (1987), Mid Cap Value (1998), Janus Fund (1970) and Janus Twenty (1985). The annual returns for all four Janus funds were similar (within 2% points) and all four were greater than that reported to Madoff investors.

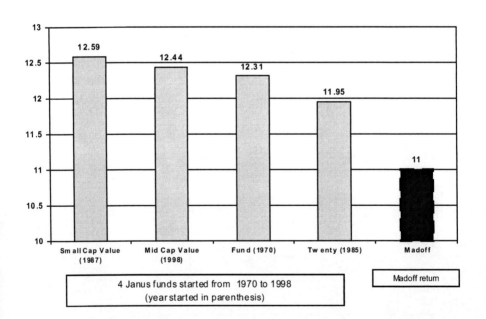

Janus Mutual Funds
Average Annual Return

Returns reported on Vanguard.com website, November 2009

Madoff Returns Versus Vanguard Mutual Funds.

Four Vanguard Funds were selected for comparison. These four funds were started from 1958 to 1984 and include Prime Cap (1984), Windsor (1958), Wellesley Income (1970) and 500 Index (1976). The Vanguard 500 Index was deliberately selected since, as an unmanaged index, it is a surrogate for the average long-term return one might expect by investing in the market. The annual returns for all four Vanguard funds were similar (within 3% points) and only the 500 Index and Wellesley Income returned less than that reported to Madoff investors.

Vanguard Mutual Funds
Average Annual Return

Returns reported on Vanguard.com website, November 2009

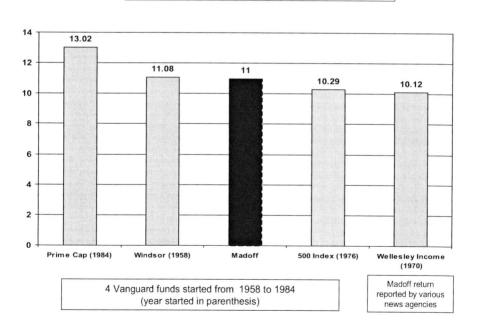

Prime Cap (1984)	Windsor (1958)	Madoff	500 Index (1976)	Wellesley Income (1970)
13.02	11.08	11	10.29	10.12

4 Vanguard funds started from 1958 to 1984 (year started in parenthesis)

Madoff return reported by various news agencies

SUMMARY

Is An 11% Annual Return Unreasonable?

The above charts show that the return reported by Madoff for the majority of his investor accounts (not including the 244 "special" accounts) were in line with those that could have been received by depositing that money with four large mutual fund companies and allowing those investments to grow over time. Indeed, Vanguard Index 500 and Wellesley Income are the only funds that performed at a lower level than that reported to Madoff investors for their accounts, and that was by less than 1 percentage point.

Therefore, the returns reported by Madoff were in line with those that an investor might reasonably expect by investing in the market for the long term. Indeed, Madoff likely deliberately reported such a comparable level of return so as not to alarm investors with unreasonably high returns that might raise questions amongst his investors.

Why did they invest with Madoff? Not because of the high rate of return, but because of the safety and predictability promised by his "advanced trading strategy."

Should Madoff Investors Have Been Suspicious About The Trading In Their Accounts?

All Madoff direct investors received transactions confirmations whenever Madoff executed trades and received monthly account statements. These statements showed stock and Treasury Bill transactions for large cap stocks that actually traded on the exchange.

The individual investor would not be alarmed by the rate of return, nor by the types of trades that were supposedly executed. The individual investor would not have the power or authority to go to Madoff's office and examine his books to determine if those trades actually occurred. Only the SEC had that power – and they failed to use it appropriately leading to the largest Ponzi scheme crime in the history of the nation and the world.

Michael De Vita
President
EDP Services, Inc
Advanced Statistical Analysis and Marketing Research Firm

Michael De Vita has over 35 years of market research experience. His experience includes working on the academic team that developed many of the advanced multivariate techniques in general use today. He has been involved in every facet of complex marketing research projects, both qualitative and quantitative.

Mike assisted in the development and application of many advanced multivariate techniques developed in the early 70's through the late 1980's. Included in these offerings are conjoint measurement, perceptual mapping and cluster analysis. He played the role of not only using but writing much of this software and therefore has the unique perspective of both a developer and practitioner of these techniques.

In addition to utilizing advanced statistical techniques on a daily basis he was a frequent guest lecturer at the University of Pennsylvania working with students taking courses for advanced degrees in marketing and statistics. He has conducted and supervised research that covers a broad range of topics, including tracking, brand image, brand positioning, customer satisfaction, loyalty, and market share projections.

Exhibits

PORTFOLIO MANAGEMENT REPORT AS OF 12/31/04   **

THIS REPORT IS PROVIDED TO ASSIST YOU IN EVALUATING THE PERFORMANCE OF YOUR
ACCOUNT AND SHOULD NOT BE USED FOR INCOME TAX PURPOSES.

STARTING EQUITY FOR CURRENT YEAR
CAPITAL ADDITIONS
CAPITAL WITHDRAWALS
REALIZED P/L FOR CURRENT YEAR
UNREALIZED P/L ON OPEN SECURITY POSITIONS
CURRENT CASH BALANCE
NET MARKET VALUE OF OPEN SECURITIES POSITIONS
TOTAL EQUITY

ANNUALIZED RETURN FOR CURRENT YEAR   10.58 %

PORTFOLIO MANAGEMENT REPORT AS OF 12/31/05   **

THIS REPORT IS PROVIDED TO ASSIST YOU IN EVALUATING THE PERFORMANCE OF YOUR
ACCOUNT AND SHOULD NOT BE USED FOR INCOME TAX PURPOSES.

STARTING EQUITY FOR CURRENT YEAR
CAPITAL ADDITIONS
CAPITAL WITHDRAWALS
REALIZED P/L FOR CURRENT YEAR
UNREALIZED P/L ON OPEN SECURITY POSITIONS
CURRENT CASH BALANCE
NET MARKET VALUE OF OPEN SECURITIES POSITIONS
TOTAL EQUITY

ANNUALIZED RETURN FOR CURRENT YEAR   9.82 %

This is a copy of the annualized statement Madoff investors would
receive at the end of the year.

Please examine the accompanying statement carefully.

Our accountants are making their regular examination of our financial records. If this statement does not agree with your records, please report any differences to our accountants:

> Friehling and Horowitz, C.P.A.'s, P.C.
> Four High Tor Road
> New City, New York 10956

You need not respond if the stated amount is accurate. However, should you find any discrepancy, an addressed envelope is enclosed for your convenience. If no differences are reported to our accountants, the accompanying statement will be considered correct.

Many innocent investors were reassured by this notice from Madoff's CPA.

BERNARD L. MADOFF
INVESTMENT SECURITIES LLC
New York □ London

DUPLICATE FOR ACCOUNT

885 Third Avenue
New York, NY 10022
(212) 230-2424
800 334-1343
(212) 838-4061

Madoff Securities Intern
12
Mayfair, Lc

6/30/07

DATE	BOUGHT RECEIVED	SOLD DELIVERED	TRN	DESCRIPTION	PRICE OR SYMBOL	AMOUNT DEBITED TO YOUR ACCOUNT	
6/26		196	26707	MORGAN STANLEY	87.640		
6/26		1,540	30984	MICROSOFT CORP	30.200		
6/26		280	37003	ABBOTT LABORATORIES	54.160		
6/26		462	41279	AMERICAN INTL GROUP INC	71.930		
6/26		294	43815	PEPSICO INC	65.920		
6/26		798	45556	BANK OF AMERICA	50.050		
6/26		1,260	48092	PFIZER INC	25.800		
6/26		968	49833	CITI GROUP INC	53.490		
6/26		560	52369	PROCTER & GAMBLE CO	62.200		
6/26		560	54102	COMCAST CORP CL A	28.380		
6/26		210	56646	SCHLUMBERGER LTD	85.630		
6/26		294	58378	CONOCOPHILIPS	79.720		
6/26		1,106	60923	AT&T INC	39.770		
6/26		1,078	62655	CISCO SYSTEMS INC	27.240		
6/26		518	65200	VERIZON COMMUNICATIONS	42.570		
6/26		378	66932	CHEVRON CORP	82.660		
6/26		336	69477	WACHOVIA CORP NEW	53.300		
6/26		1,820	71209	GENERAL ELECTRIC CO	38.890		
6/26		602	73754	WELLS FARGO & CO NEW	35.680		
6/26		42	75486	GOOGLE	513.770		
6/26		434	78031	WAL-MART STORES INC	48.660		
6/26		70	79763	GOLDMAN SACHS GROUP INC	225.860		
6/26		1,008	82308	EXXON MOBIL CORP	84.400		
6/26		364	83994	HOME DEPOT INC	40.060		

CONTINUED ON PAGE 4

This is a copy of a page from a monthly statement received by Madoff investors showing the type of stocks he "traded" in. While these looked very real, in fact Madoff never made a single trade.

SEC (Securities and Exchange Commission)

"The mission of the U.S. Securities and Exchange Commission is to protect investors, maintain fair, orderly, and efficient markets, and facilitate capital formation."
http://www.sec.gov/about/whatwedo.shtml

SEC's Inspector General H. David Kotz Report # 509, August 31, 2009.

"**Background:** On December 11, 2008, the Securities and Exchange
Commission (SEC) charged Bernard L. Madoff (Madoff) with securities fraud for a multi-billion dollar Ponzi scheme that he perpetrated on advisory clients of his firm. Subsequently, the Commission learned that credible and specific allegations regarding Madoff's financial wrongdoing, going back to at least 1999, were repeatedly brought to the attention of SEC staff but were never recommended to the Commission for action."
http://www.sec-oig.gov/Reports/AuditsInspections/2009/467.pdf

Investigation of Failure of the SEC to Uncover Bernard Madoff's Ponzi Scheme.

"On August 31, 2009, the OIG issued a comprehensive, 450-plus page investigative report, *Investigation of Failure of the SEC to Uncover Bernard Madoff's Ponzi Scheme*, Report No. 509. The investigation found that the SEC received more than ample information in the form of detailed and substantive complaints over a period of many years to warrant a thorough and comprehensive examination and/or investigation of Bernard Madoff and Bernard Madoff Investment Securities, LLC (BMIS) for operating a Ponzi scheme. However, despite three examinations and two

investigations of Madoff and BMIS, a thorough and competent investigation or examination was never performed, and the SEC never identified the Ponzi scheme that Madoff operated."
http://www.sec-oig.gov/Reports/AuditsInspections/2009/470.pdf

The Role Of SIPC (Securities Investor Protection Corporation)

"SIPC is the first line of defense in the event a brokerage firm fails owing customers cash and securities that are missing from customer accounts. Although not every investor is protected by SIPC, no fewer than 99 percent of persons who are eligible get their investments back from SIPC. From its creation by Congress in 1970 through December 2008, SIPC advanced $520 million in order to make possible the recovery of $160.0 billion in assets for an estimated 761,000 investors. When a brokerage is closed due to bankruptcy or other financial difficulties and customer assets are missing, SIPC steps in as quickly as possible and, within certain limits, works to return customers' cash, stock and other securities. Without SIPC, investors at financially troubled brokerage firms might lose their securities or money forever…or wait for years while their assets are tied up in court. However, because not everyone, and not every loss, is protected by SIPC, you are urged to read this whole brochure carefully to learn about the limits of protection."
http://www.sipc.org/how/brochure.cfm#six

SIPA (Securities Investor Protection Act)

"The SIPA is codified in Title 15 of the United States Code at Sections 78aaa - 111. The SIPA created the SIPC, a nonprofit, private membership corporation to which most registered brokers and dealers are required to belong. 15 U.S.C. § 78ccc. The SIPC fund, which constitutes an insurance program, is authorized under

226

15 U.S.C. § 78ddd(a), and assessments against members are authorized by 15 U.S.C. §§ 78ddd(c) and (d). The fund is designed to protect the customers of brokers or dealers subject to the SIPA from loss in case of financial failure of the member. The fund is supported by assessments upon its members. If the fund should become inadequate, the SIPA authorizes borrowing against the U.S. Treasury. An analogy could be made to the role of the Federal Deposit Insurance Corporation in the banking industry."

http://www.uscourts.gov/bankruptcycourts/bankruptcybasics/sipa.html#sipa

FINRA (Financial Industry Regulatory Authority)

"The Financial Industry Regulatory Authority (FINRA) is the largest independent regulator for all securities firms doing business in the United States. All told, FINRA oversees nearly 4,750 brokerage firms, about 167,000 branch offices and approximately 634,000 registered securities representatives.Created in July 2007 through the consolidation of NASD and the member regulation, enforcement and arbitration functions of the New York Stock Exchange, FINRA is dedicated to investor protection and market integrity through effective and efficient regulation and complementary compliance and technology-based services."
http://www.finra.org/AboutFINRA/index.html

Broker/Dealer

"FINRA firms that act as securities dealers or brokers, or perform both functions."
http://www.finra.org